WALK THROUGH THE WILDERNESS

A WALK THROUGH THE WILDERNESS

ONE MAN'S JOURNEY
FROM FAITH TO FUNDAMENTALISM TO ATHEISM

Dear Herb & Shirley
 You believed in me at a time in my life when I needed to be believed in. I'll never forget that.
  love

DAN CONGER

atmosphere press

© 2022 Dan Conger

Published by Atmosphere Press

Cover design by Matthew Fielder

No part of this book may be reproduced without permission from the author except in brief quotations and in reviews.

atmospherepress.com

I'm eighteen years old, and I'm standing in Cottonwood Plaza, Bishop, California. This is my last day living here. Memories flood my mind. Nostalgia for days now past and trepidation for my unknown future compete for prominence in my thinking. At any moment my eighteen-year-old self is going to leave town and I won't be returning. I'm heading off to college at Humboldt State University in extreme northwestern California on the redwood coast, and I'm on the cusp of independent manhood. As I stand here, 14,246-foot-tall White Mountain Peak looms to the northeast. The winter of 1994–1995 brought heavy snows (a record at the time), and now in late August as I prepare to leave my hometown to pursue my own adult life, there are still significant snowfields near

White Mountain Peak

the summit. Looking at this gorgeous mountain I think to myself, "One day, I'll be back, and I'll live here."

I was so naïve and idealistic ... even when compared to other teens leaving home for the first time. As an example, I never even visited Humboldt State University before applying for admittance. The university was chosen simply because it was small, located in a similarly small town, and had reasonably easy access to wilderness areas close by. Choosing a university without ever visiting it or the larger area around it resulted in no small degree of culture shock later when I arrived. In my mind, the only important factors were "small town" and "near mountains." The fact that it rained nearly forty inches every year and when it wasn't rainy it was often foggy to the point that the sky was essentially melting onto the world below? Never even took those things into consideration.

My naïvety and idealism would come to get me into quite a situation. I would never have imagined that in a few short weeks I would become involved in a controlling and abusive fundamentalist cult that would dominate every aspect of my life for nearly a decade. This group would redirect the course of my life in ways I never could have dreamed of and leave me so emotionally scarred that years of slow recovery would ensue. Having said that, my experience was not among the worst that people went through as part of this group, so I think actually I had it relatively easy. No matter how easy it was compared to some others in the cult, however, the emotional toll on me was profound and has had a lasting impact on my life. Today, I am fully recovered and value the lessons learned in those years, but I must be bluntly honest about the reality of what *was* in the group.

Since I intend to be very honest about what was, there is one note I need to make very clear here at the outset. As I relate experiences in the group, it is unavoidable that I will mention abusive acts from cult leadership and other members. Hell, I was guilty of verbally abusing people in the group myself, so it would be silly and more than a little hypocritical of me to throw stones at others when I could easily be hit by those same stones thrown my way. When bringing these things up, it is inevitable that the memories will cause some amount of emotional distress for others. As a result, I need to say quite plainly that *all* of the former leaders of my home Assembly in Arcata have entirely repented in the truest sense of the word. They know they hurt people and have (in my opinion) taken every reasonable action they can to make things right with those they injured. Repentance is real for all of them. Let the reader bear in mind that as I relate these experiences, I am in no way attempting to crucify these people all over again. Having said that, it is impossible to describe these things without former Arcata Assembly members (as well as those from other cities) recognizing each other. Understand that I am not telling these stories to make accusations or to cause further harm. This is my recollection and description of events, and it is meant to tell my story, not cast stones at or condemn anyone.

I've given tremendous thought to my time in this group in the nearly twenty years since its worldwide collapse. What so attracted me? Why did I ignore the obvious problems? How did the group's leadership convince me to so thoroughly abandon almost every sense of rationality in favor of dogma? Finally, why on earth did

I continue working towards the success of the group for more than a year after the truth had been laid bare? Reflecting on my involvement now, I can see in utter clarity how I was truly lost in the wilderness. The irony there is that while in the group I thought it was everyone else that was lost. I really thought I knew where I was going. I truly believed that I had *the* Truth. Now I can see that I was just wandering aimlessly in the dark. I assumed I knew where my destination was. In reality, I did not.

This is my story. One man's journey through the darkness, all the while believing he was walking in ultimate light. How did it start? How did it end? How did I recover? Where am I now?

The reader is welcome to come along on this walk through the wilderness with me.

Chapter One
Who Am I Anyway?

I was raised in a middle-class family. My father is now retired from thirty years in law enforcement, having served in the Navy submarine corps before that, and my mother was a homemaker. I have one sister who is younger by 2¾ years. Today, she and I are estranged. We attended church nearly every Sunday, grew up going to Sunday School, and I was raised in a faith-filled environment. However, that faith was very liberal with no basis at all in biblical literalism or extremism of any kind. The Bible, it was explained, was mostly symbolic. Messages like, "Love your neighbor as you love yourself," and, "Do unto others as you would have them do unto you," were the important things. All of the killing, genocide, slavery, and other judgments of God ... these were not to be taken seriously or literally. Rather, they were to be seen as symbolic stories told to communicate a deeper message, or mere records of historical events like a textbook, rather than literal moral teachings to be taken at face value. We attended large national church conventions and other regional religious gatherings and were involved in youth groups.

All in all, life was good.

We lived in Canoga Park, California, from the time I

was born in 1977 until August 1991. My parents had purchased our Los Angeles area home a couple of years prior to my birth. We enjoyed living there, although it was crowded and the sky was often so smoggy that participating in swimming and other forms of exercise made my lungs hurt. As a child, however, you don't notice these things too much. You just run and play and catch and chase. So long as there is ample food on the table, there are fun games to be had, and generous love in one's family, that is all that matters.

It was certainly all that mattered to me.

I knew when I came home, no matter what had happened at school, I would be loved and cared for. However, the pollution affected me so much that I eventually developed a mild form of asthma. Breathing deeply resulted in extreme pain and bouts of intense coughing. How could I run around outdoors and play if I couldn't even breathe properly? To illustrate how bad the air could get during the eighties and nineties, to the northeast of downtown Los Angeles about forty-five miles is a 10,000-foot-tall mountain called Mt. Baldy. The smog is so bad on many days that this massive mountain can't even be seen through the haze from downtown LA. Quite literally, on a bad smog day, the sight in the picture above is completely invisible and all that is seen is a wall of grayish-brown nastiness in the air. During the period of time when I was growing up there, smog banks would move in. Not fog banks ... smog banks.

As a very active child, I was involved in soccer and track & field. Between those outdoor sports and my love of swimming, I was always breathing the bad air quite deeply, and this is what resulted in my case of childhood asthma. Climbing out of a pool, I would find that my lungs just would not expand all the way, like a balloon trapped inside of a box. No matter how hard one tries, the walls of the box prevent the balloon from inflating fully. It would leave me gasping and suffocated and in pain all at once.

As an escape from the crowds and pollution, we loved taking camping trips in the local mountains to locations like Mt. Piños and Big Bear, as well as more extended outdoor trips to Bishop, Mammoth, and Yosemite. Some of my fondest childhood memories are of sitting in the woods near Tuolumne Meadows in Yosemite National Park, the Tuolumne River babbling away nearby as crystal clear waters rolled and boiled over rocks and cascaded down falls. My parents would sit there and read *The Chronicles of Narnia* and *The Hobbit* aloud in this amazing natural landscape. Images of the wonderful creatures in these tales would dance in my mind, and I would imagine them running through the woods, or dancing across the river with their flutes. Hearing these stories read aloud in this environment, I imagined that a talking beaver would emerge from those waters and lead me off on some wild adventure! This reading, and this imagining, was deeply formative for me as a child. Even when not reading the stories aloud, my imagination would still run wild every time I ventured out into the great outdoors. Was Smaug the Golden sitting in a cave somewhere up on that great mountain peak? Was Mr. Tumnus just around the corner with his magic flute? Would I, on some hike through the high country, come across a troop of dwarves returning from some great mining adventure deeper in the mountains? For a child, these fantasies conjure in the mind easily when exposed to the works of C. S. Lewis and J. R. R. Tolkien in a natural place as amazing as the Sierra Nevada. Given the amount of time I spent in the mountains being exposed to such stories, it is no wonder that I grew up to love the natural world.

I was involved in our extended family and spent lots of time with grandparents, aunts, uncles, and cousins. My sister and I were the youngest of all the cousins, so we were doted on by everyone in the family. Scholastically, I was an average student. I did not particularly excel in any subject, partly because I was so easily distracted by just about anything. My mind would wander incessantly (and often it still does), and I had a hard time paying attention for long periods of time, especially in a classroom setting. My biology teacher in middle school would be droning on about photosynthesis, and my mind would be strapped to skis on some high slope tearing through powder. In addition, I was not a "cool" kid, either. In seventh and eighth grade, I was shorter than most boys, skinny as a rail, and very socially awkward. I was mercilessly picked on and dreaded every day. Fortunately, I had a friend in middle school who was one year ahead of me. He looked after me somewhat. Despite all his faults (including his occasional participation in my humiliation), he was like the big brother I never had, and although I was still picked on, he made sure I was never beat up or truly hurt.

Thanks, Bobby.

As I approached high school age, my parents decided that they did not want us going to school in the LA area any longer. There was too much opportunity for us to be corrupted by various forms of crime, and the pollution was still wreaking havoc on my lungs. Not only did we regularly vacation in California's Sierra Nevada, but we had family living in the small town of Bishop on the east side of the mountain range. My parents decided to move there to get us out of the city and into the clean small-town environment. So, when August of 1991 arrived, we departed Los Angeles. Instead of living in the smog and crowds of the San Fernando Valley and attending a high school with upwards of three thousand students, I would now be living at six thousand feet and attending a high school with six hundred students. As of the 2018 census, the town population was 3,746. Consider that fact for just a brief moment ... the entire population of the town we were moving to was only slightly larger than the number of students at the high school I would have attended in Chatsworth, California.

Life would be *very* different in this small town.

I had vacationed in this area since I was a small child, and now I lived in our favorite vacation spot. Remember how any little thing distracted me in the Los Angeles area? Yeah, my grades actually went down in Bishop even though my stress level was lower. We were ninety minutes from Yosemite, sixty minutes from Mammoth Mountain Ski Area, and some of the most glorious fishing lakes on the east side of the Sierra were just ten minutes from the house. Upon hopping onto mountain bikes, I could ride away from the house onto a dirt road and be surrounded by wilderness without another soul in sight in just minutes. If I had trouble focusing on school in Los Angeles, now that I lived on the edge of the wilderness the words "trouble focusing" came nowhere near doing my distraction justice.

I recall one day I was running around the high desert with new friends, and we happened upon a mostly devoured *fresh* deer carcass. Upon returning home, I informed our parents of our discovery and my dad wanted to see it. My sister and I (ages twelve and fourteen, respectively) walked back out there with him to the site, not even considering the fact that it was nearly dusk, and this time I noticed something that I hadn't previously. There were gigantic pawprints all around the area. My father could put his hand into the prints, and they were larger than his outspread fingers.

It was a mountain lion kill ... and it had been made recently.

Walking home, my dad had us walk single file with me in front, and him in the back. We retraced our steps back to the house, and I noticed there were huge pawprints following our original tracks out to the deer kill site. My heart pounding, and genuinely fearing we were in danger as dusk deepened, we walked the rest of the way home. Back at the house, heart still racing, I told my father about the tracks and he said he had noticed them, too. We had been followed by the lion, he suspected, back out to the site of the deer carcass, and the lion had likely followed us back to the house again. It was our first interaction with the natural dangers of our new home. We had been so taken by the natural wonders that the natural dangers there didn't even enter our thinking.

Another experience my dad and I had the next spring

was to drive out to the local climbing rocks in the Buttermilks and go for a climb together. As we parked the truck, a buck came charging past the vehicle so close it nearly hit us. The reason the deer almost hit us? It was looking back over its shoulder as it ran. My dad and I talked about how amazing it was, and then went on our hike. There is no established trail where we were, so we forged our own way through the sagebrush. We had a great time, doing something of a loop hike where we rejoined our tracks about four hundred yards from the truck. Once again, we were greeted rather unpleasantly by the sight of huge pawprints following our footprints out on the loop we had just taken. Frozen in place, my dad and I looked at each other and almost simultaneously said, "The deer ..." We surmised that the deer had narrowly escaped the lion, resulting in its panicked charge past the truck, and then the lion had turned and followed us. Although we understood that lions normally follow people out of curiosity rather than for hunting, it still shook us. When we were out and about, we needed to have our wits about us.

The most profound discovery in this area for me, however, came the summer after we moved there. I jumped on my mountain bike and headed out with some friends. We rode up and down the dirt roads and across meadows and through creeks, water splashing and dust kicking up, all with the massive mountain peaks looming nearby. "Hey," said my friend Trevor. "Do you want to see the waterfall?" Wait, waterfall? "YES!!!" I replied. Deep in the Buttermilks near my hometown was a magical place, and this place of wonder was where they were now taking me.

No, I won't tell you where it is.

We ditched our bikes near the top of a steep sandy slope that dropped down into a grotto surrounded by rounded rocks and scrubby desert pines mixed with aspen. A few inches deep, the sand sits atop the solid granite rock below. It is more slippery than ice. As I carefully descended from foothold to foothold on this steep slope, the sound of crashing water slowly grew. The small creek here flowed noisily through the bottom of the grotto. Upon reaching the bottom, we turned a corner and I saw it. Falling roughly fifteen feet from one level of the grotto to the next, the waterfall roared away. Spring snow melt having swelled the normally small creek, the site was breathtaking. Only twenty feet apart, granite walls rose on both sides soaring up about a hundred feet. Air moved through the grotto between those stone cliffs and stirred the mists created by the short fall of water. Fed by the Humphreys Glaciers, the water was extraordinarily cold. However, in the hot dry desert that frigid water was quite a relief. I can't tell you how many times I've waded in that little alcove beneath the towering granite, resting on the small shelf of rock beside the falls. This place became a refuge that I would go to, and one to which I still love to return.

No, I already told you, I'm not telling you where it is!

I absolutely loved Bishop (my parents are now retired there in the same home we moved to in 1991). One could go to the grocery store and know the name of the grocers, and they would know yours. Overall, there was a friendly small-town atmosphere. Best of all, there were the mountains. Only a few short miles to the west of our house rose mountains that topped out at just under fourteen thousand feet. Snowy winters, wildflower-laden springs, hot high desert summers, autumns of golden trees, thunderstorms, fishing, mountain biking, rock climbing, skiing ... an

Western view from my parents' home

all-you-can-eat buffet of outdoor activities and ZERO smog to hurt our lungs (barring occasional smoke from summer forest fires). Quite literally, my asthma was completely gone within a few short weeks of living there. No more searing pain when exercising. No more coughing fits. Done. I continued carrying an inhaler but really didn't need it unless I became ill with some type of respiratory infection.

Today I am completely asthma-free.

The high school years passed as they do for any other teenager. I had my growing pains, made my mistakes, hurt people and was hurt in return, learned my lessons, and got ready to get out into the world on my own. One theme that was true for me was that I always looked for belonging. I wanted to be "cool" and "popular." I sought ways to fit in, but the more I tried the more fake I became and the more I failed. This intense desire to fit in with a group—to *belong* somehow—would play a significant role in my early adulthood.

By the time 1994 came around and I was wrapping up my junior year, I seriously began considering my future for the first time. What would I do once I was done with high school? Sure, I would go to college, but to learn what ... and *do* what after that? I wanted to make a difference in the world, not just do some job until retirement and then die. I wanted a life that meant something more. During my teenage years, the pastor of the United Methodist Church in Bishop was really inspiring to me. His words touched people. He actually cared, and he didn't play to politics or personalities. The congregation knew he was not just preaching, but he actually *cared* about them. It was at age seventeen during the early part of my senior year that I determined I would become a pastor like him. I would learn how to reach people, teach people, and change lives for the better. I wanted to know God in a deeper and more meaningful way.

Then, on January 1, 1995, during the middle of my senior year of high school, I made a New Year's resolution that I would read the entire Bible from cover to cover. I had heard stories from the Bible since I was a child, even participating in church plays and being a part of the choir. Starting in Genesis, I decided I would read straight through to the end of Revelation. I was faithful to this resolution and began reading regularly. As anyone who has read the early books of the Old Testament can tell you, they are full of stories of faithfulness versus faithlessness ... judgment versus reward. In addition, they are full of stories of God's will being done with no regard for whether a person is faithful or not (the book of Job, anybody?). In general, however, those who were faithful would be rewarded. Those who were faithless would be judged. For those who did not respond to God's holy discipline, incredible punishment was reserved ... even death.

As I was reading these things, an event took place that changed my perspective on life and spirituality radically.

Mammoth Mountain Ski Area did something special for local school students while I lived in Bishop. Local kids could ski for $1/day. Yes, you read that right. No typo ... a full day lift ticket, any day of the week, including weekends and holidays ... $1/day. If you were on your high school ski racing team, like I was, then you got a free season pass.

I skied my brains out.

I averaged about fifty ski days per season for my four years of high school. By the time I was a senior, I had become quite the expert skier. Frozen wind in my hair flying off a cornice and landing in waist-deep snow ... heaven on earth. Then, on March 4th, 1995, I was standing atop Dave's Run on Mammoth Mountain's summit ridge. We were supposed to be training for our ski race team state championships which were soon coming, but some friends and I decided to go take advantage of some fresh snow. To get an idea of the scale of this run, there are a few tiny skiers in this photo that you can pick out if you look closely. That week, a huge storm had dumped nine feet of snow on the mountain in only two days. It was epic!

High winds had come up that day in March, and they had created a gigantic cornice at the apex of Dave's Run. In the photo above, you can clearly see the cornice wrapping around the summit ridge and casting quite a shadow. Three friends and I were there, with the wind roaring and blowing snow in billowing curtains off the summit ridge. Normally, getting to Dave's from the summit gondola required quite a bit of work with skating and poll pushing. That day, however, howling winds over the summit allowed us to stick our arms out and simply be blown along the summit ridge to the run like sailboats being blown across the ocean. On that day in 1995, I intended to leap off of this massive cornice. I had done this many times before on various runs at Mammoth. Today, though, would be the largest I had attempted to date. It would be an approximately forty-foot drop.

Mammoth is one part of a dormant supervolcano called Long Valley Caldera. The caldera crater is twenty-two miles long (west to east) and seventeen miles wide (north to south). Mammoth Mountain sits on the western rim of this massive caldera. Small swarms of earthquakes at very shallow depth are quite common. I didn't know it at the time, but as I stood there on the top of this massive cornice getting ready to make my drop, a small earthquake at very shallow depth occurred directly beneath Mammoth Mountain. This small quake combined with my weight caused the cornice to collapse under my feet, and I was swept away in an avalanche.

Rather than jumping the massive cornice heroically, I watched in horror as the ground beneath my feet fractured. The break spread through the snow along the edge of the ridge both to my left and right, as well as under my skis, in a widening crack that opened up just a few inches behind my ski boots, much like a zipper quickly unzipping, leaving only the tails of my skis on terra firma. Since most of my weight was now over open air, gravity did its inexorable thing. A sense of weightlessness gripped me as the frozen ground dropped away under my feet. Some asshole, somewhere in time and space, hit the slow-motion time-lapse button on my life and the next few seconds played out like some sick scene from a horror movie. The widening crack suddenly released as the cornice broke away. I was unaware of it at the time, but the entirety of the cornice had broken loose, and the massive blocks of snow and ice were now falling out from under my feet towards the main slope. I would not be jumping the approximately forty feet to the steep slope below like a superhero. I would be plummeting with gigantic blocks of hardened snow and ice impacting mere micro-seconds before I did.

As I slid forward and over the edge, I flailed my arms about for a moment trying to prevent the inexorable pull of the singularity in front of me, but to no avail. The cornice slammed into the main slope with a thundering roar, and plumes of snow erupted outward from the site of impact ... a site of impact that I was now swiftly falling toward. As I fell, I remember being off-balance in the air, leaning slightly leftward and forward, but I managed to kick off the wall of the cornice during my plummet and actually landed on my feet. However, since my feet touched down on a slope that was in motion and swiftly racing down the face of the mountain, I fell flat on my face and began sliding on my chest with my feet scorpioning over my back. My spine twisted intensely as I imagined my own ski-booted feet kicking me in the back of the head, and I had the panicked feeling that any moment I was just going to snap in half like a pencil being snapped under the thumb of a body builder. When the pain reached a crescendo that I thought I couldn't endure any longer, somehow, I was rolled over onto my back again with my feet below me and I noticed gigantic blocks of snow rolling all around me (I later learned that the ski patrol calls these large rolling blocks "death cookies"). The clouds of snow in the air hit my face and lungs like millions of tiny razor blades. A sense of resignation took hold of me and I thought, "This is how it ends for me," while the world roiled all around.

A few lingering echoes.

Silence.

As suddenly as the mayhem erupted, peace descended over the mountain.

I found myself lying on my back, partially covered by avalanche debris. Clouds drifted lazily in the beautiful Sierra sky, and lingering clouds of floating snow crystals drifted out of the air around me. Downslope from the summit, I was semi-protected from the high winds over the crest. Later, my three friends who were with me would tell me that the whole thing lasted perhaps four seconds. Didn't feel that way to me. That asshole I mentioned earlier had hit the slo-mo feature on my life, so it was seemingly hours of tormented fear for me. Seemed like an eternity of terrifying hell that would never end. In the end, however, the regular speed button was activated and the world returned to normal. Ski patrol quickly arrived on the scene and began probing the avalanche debris for other victims. Of myself and my three friends present that day, I was the only one caught up, although one of them (I mentioned Trevor earlier when discussing the waterfall a few miles from our home) was actually downslope when it started and only escaped by quickly skiing laterally across the slope to get out of the way.

Thankfully, there were no other victims.

This event changed my life in a pretty significant way. You see, as I had been reading the Bible it had been making me feel guilty about certain things in my life. I wasn't a bad kid. I was just making normal teenage decisions, which the Bible frowns upon. My eighteen-year-old mind concluded that God was trying to tell me something. I had been reading about how God would pour judgment upon people. If they turned and repented, God gave them favor. If they didn't repent, things went from bad to worse really quickly. I concluded that the same God I was reading about in the Old Testament was saying to me, "Shape up, or else!!!" The avalanche was not just some random freak event. It was a direct message from the Almighty to my teenage self. I fell to my knees right there on the slope, and in tears silently prayed to God that I would be faithful to him. I had prayed for my salvation and been born again when I was fourteen but didn't really change anything about my teenage life and choices. Although I was raised a liberal Christian with a very liberal theology, the seeds of fundamentalism had just been planted ... and they immediately took root. Faithless rebel I would no longer be. Faithful servant I would become. My pledge to become a pastor had just taken a new tone, and I began taking things utterly seriously. I still made many teenage decisions that at the time provoked more than a little guilt, but always in my mind was this idea that I would one day become the servant of the Almighty.

I continued reading through the Old Testament during the remainder of my high school months, and increasingly took a literalist view of what I read. Of course, I ignored the heinous crimes of genocide, slavery, and misogyny that I read there, and excused it as God punishing wicked people or just something symbolic (commit genocide against the impurity in your immortal soul, for example). You see, he had warned me by allowing the avalanche to nearly kill me, and I had repented. These people? If it was a literal story, there must have been some wanton wickedness about them that had required their merciless slaughter, I reasoned.

During my final summer in Bishop, most of my friends left town before I did, so I was almost the last man standing. I did more fishing, hiking, biking, and climbing that summer than any summer prior because some part of me knew I would never live there, nor would I have this opportunity, again. As a bonus, that ski season of 1994–1995 had Mammoth's longest on record. The resort opened on October 8th, 1994, and didn't close ski operations until August 13th, 1995, due to the phenomenal snowpack that year. My summer, therefore, had quite a bit of skiing in it as well. I didn't work, although my parents really wanted me to, because I was too busy trying to live up every last moment of outdoor adventure before leaving. Crashing through creeks on my mountain bike. Hiking up to backcountry glaciers with their glacial lakes. Ski mountaineering and skiing at Mammoth. Clean, dry air filling my lungs and blowing across my face. Eagles soaring in the skies above.

Finally, that moment came. Time had mercilessly progressed and departure was at hand. We packed up everything into two cars and drove off late one hot August afternoon. We would take a couple of days traveling the vast distance to Arcata and Humboldt State University. We took the time partly because it was a thirteen-hour drive when taken in one shot, and partly to spend some final moments together as a nuclear family. The drive from Bishop to Arcata is amazingly gorgeous on every last mile of highway. Up the Eastern Sierra and that glorious mountain range, through the southern Cascades and Lassen National Park, past Mt. Shasta, and then through California's northern coastal ranges along the Trinity River. That drive is singularly beautiful, and there are times that I actually miss making the thirteen-hour haul from Arcata to Bishop.

Upon arriving in Arcata, the coastal fog hugged the Pacific and rolled up into the redwood-covered hills. Just forty-five minutes from Arcata, in the town of Willow Creek, it had been 95 degrees on the Trinity River. Now it was about fifty-five and we all broke out our jeans and sweaters. My mind was spinning a little from that first shock. "Wait," I thought, "isn't this August? Isn't this supposed to be summer? Is it like this here all the time???" Upon arriving, we took a brief driving tour around campus and through the hippie center of the universe ... I mean, Arcata (think Berkeley, California, times ten thousand). Despite the wet cold fog, the town plaza was covered with hippies. Dreadlocks, bongo drums, tie-dye, guitars and singing, pipes filled with a certain herb ... it was all everywhere. I was suffering from such a profound degree of culture shock that I was almost lost for words (I could talk the head off of a horse, so being lost for words is rare for me). Remember, I had never even visited Humboldt County or toured the college in preparation for my arrival. We had a very nice dinner at a restaurant in the Jacoby Storehouse, and ate some ice cream at the parlor downstairs.

The next day dawned bright and clear. We got a taste of what the weather was like in Humboldt County when it was good ... and *boy* was it good when it was good. On a nice Humboldt day, the temperature is 75 degrees, there is barely any breeze, the sky is crystal clear and bright blue, and the deep green redwood forests march their way up into the coastal mountains. Most of the fall is like this in Humboldt, and that is the season that makes it worth living there. I finished the initial setup of my dorm room and got ready to say goodbye to my family. The week ahead was orientation, so there would be no classes. Just time to settle in.

I never got the license plate of the truck that hit me at that moment, but the impact hammered me hard. I was saying goodbye. This was it. I was now going to be on my own. A fog descended on my mind much like the fog that descends on those forests.

My father handed me a rather large check, told me to go open a bank account and then go get a job. The check was for books, tuition, and just to get me started. After that, they would pay for my tuition, books, rent, dorm meal bills, and a few other things ... everything else was on me. He gave me a hug, told me how proud he was of me, and then walked away. Mom gave me a big hug. She really did a good job keeping it together. I stood there feeling more than a little bit in shock while I slowly realized ... wait, this is happening ... they are driving away and leaving me here. They're *really* doing it. *I'm* really doing it. I'm on my own now.

Wow. I'm not sure who took the emotional impact worst that day, but it was really rough for me.

As the car crawled down the small avenue in front of

the dorms, I saw them through the back window (no tinting in that car). Dad appeared to just be Dad. A bit stoic and concentrating on his immediate job of getting them all safely back to Bishop on that thirteen-hour drive. My mother dragged her sunglasses off of her face with her left hand and raised her right over her eyes as her shoulders began rocking with uncontrollable sobs. The back window of that little car framed the image for me. That asshat with the slow-motion button? He pressed it again while I watched them drive away.

Dad later said Mom cried most of the thirteen hours back to Bishop.

I stood there watching them go. I had just been hit by that truck, as you recall, so I couldn't really move. Just watched. Then, the car made a left and departed my field of view. I knew the freeway entrance was just out of sight, and in my mind's eye I saw the little car enter the freeway and speed off. That was it. I was a man now. The asshat with the slow-motion button hadn't reset to normal speed, so everything moved in time-lapse as I turned and walked back to my room. I didn't cry. I was a little too shocked by that. I sat on my little bed in the dorm room for a while, not sure what to do with myself. My roommate was not to arrive until later that week, so I would have some time to myself to adjust to things. It was a Sunday, so I really couldn't do anything about opening the bank account or seriously look for a job. I honestly don't know how long I sat there. I looked at my small collection of books on the bookshelf but didn't feel like reading. I didn't want to do anything on the computer, and back in 1995 computers simply were not what they are today, anyway. I really didn't want to drive anywhere, partly because I just didn't know where to go and partly because I didn't know anyone. It was a glorious clear 75-degree day in Humboldt County, without any fog or rain, and all I could do was sit there and think.

I felt so very alone in that eternal moment.

After an indeterminate amount of time, which must have been significant because the day had passed from morning into early afternoon, some others came by my room and through the window noticed me sitting there. I had met a couple of them earlier in the day. With a knock on the window and a smile, I was invited to join them for a short hike up into the woods behind the campus. The asshat with the slow-motion button chose this moment to reset life to normal speed. They were second-year students, and certainly knew something of what I must be going through. They knew of a spot (it's literally called "Stoner's Rock" by the students) to hike to right up behind the dorms by Jolly Giant Creek under the full canopy of old-growth redwood forest. I didn't have anything better to do, so I went with them. I had been to the redwoods in the greater San Francisco Bay Area, but this was my first experience in deep old-growth redwoods. The creek quietly babbled away, and we hiked along listening to the sounds of the coastal birds that nest in those forests. I probably wasn't very good company because I really didn't talk much, but I did make a couple of friends and they seemed to understand that I both needed to be quietly lost in my own thoughts, but also appreciated the company.

That night, I had dinner alone in the dorm cafeteria and pondered the future. What would I do other than look for a job during the next week? There were some events planned for the dorm residents by the management of the student residence halls. I would go ahead and participate in those, but that was just to pass the time. Maybe I would meet some Christians that I could befriend? As I was leaving the cafeteria, I noticed a posting board on the wall covered with posters for various campus clubs and other groups. Right there, in the middle of all the others was THE poster. It had an open book in the center, with rays of light shining up out of it. It said, "BIBLE STUDY, Fridays at 7 p.m., Siemen's Hall, Room 109." There were other church posters, but this one jumped out at me. Right there I decided I would go. There were little tear-offs on the bottom with the time and room number, so I took one with me.

I hadn't the first idea what I was getting myself into.

Chapter Two
Ensnared

Traps are intended to spring shut on unsuspecting victims. A well-laid trap is one where the victim isn't even aware that they are ensnared until it is far too late. In the most successful cults, the traps are so deviously designed that the very people laying them are often completely unaware that they are doing it. Such was the case for the vast majority of people involved in the Assembly, myself included. We were spoon-fed dogma, and having devoured it we then went out of our way to prepare the same meal for every other soul we could. In our hearts, nearly 100 percent of us were completely convinced that what we were doing was right and good and just and true. In our minds, this wasn't abusive or wrong in any way. It was the will of God!

How did they get me?

I kept that little tear-off from the poster and placed it on my small dorm desk. There were no iPads or iPods or i-Anythings in 1995 (hell, I didn't even buy my first cell phone until 2002), so I tracked it all on paper. Since the Bible study was not until Friday, I had all week. I went to the bank as soon as it opened Monday morning and took care of opening my first independent bank account. I then began looking for jobs. In my mind, the way to get a job was at the mall ... so off to Eureka's Bayshore Mall I went. It never occurred to me that there were jobs to be had on campus, so I drove the thirty minutes without a second thought. I actually found a job almost immediately at a new candle store that was opening up. With a sense of triumph, I then drove back to the dorms ... the job wouldn't be starting for a few weeks since That Candle Store was a brand-new retail outlet and everything was still being set up. The owner was a Christian, too, so in my mind that confirmed it was a good job to secure. Events galore took place at the dorms as various clubs and campus groups tried to get new students settled in, and recruited new members for the semester. I had fun participating in silly mock-sports events, meeting some new people, and getting ready for classes to begin the following week. As part of my pre-pastoral studies, I had declared for a philosophy major. I also made it down to a local beach and was overjoyed to find it completely free of both trash and people. Unlike Southern California beaches which are mobbed almost all year, there was almost nobody there and I could just walk in the sand while the gulls called and sea lions barked out in the surf. The days ticked by, and more and more I recovered from that truck accident that occurred when my parents left.

I still couldn't find the license plate, though.

The most fun I had was at the sand volleyball court behind one of the dorm buildings. Every evening, groups of students would gather for games and I really loved it. I met a large group of new people there. All the while, though, I was thinking about the Bible study. Out of all the people I met, I judged that almost none of them were serious Christians. Also, of the Christians I met, I judged them to be worldly and not very serious about their faith, much like I had been in high school. One of them in particular would argue biblical doctrine until the cows came home, not accepting that his opinion could even be remotely wrong, and then would run off to drink, curse, and sex it up without a second thought. As a result, despite the fact that I had met so many people and had so much fun at the volleyball court, I was longing for more deeply spiritual connections.

Slowly, the days ticked by that week and Friday finally came (remember, this was orientation week and there were no classes). I had been studying the Bible extensively in preparation for the meeting that night. I excitedly walked up the stairs behind the dorms, made it to the building where the study was to be, arrived at the room ... and it was totally dark. Not a soul anywhere. My heart just sank to the bottom of my shoes, and when it got there it kept sinking. I had been looking forward to this all week long, and nobody was there.

I was actually depressed ... about a Bible study.

Despite all the people I had met, actually finding a job in economically depressed Eureka, California, successfully registering for classes, and all in all doing a damn good job being a responsible adult ... I walked away like the sullen teenager I was (hey, I was in fact eighteen and *was* pretty sullen) and went back to my dorm room. I could have gone out somewhere, since there were students doing that, or gone to play volleyball. Nope. I sulked back to my room and just sat there. My roommate had arrived at that point, but he was out and about. I was glad he was gone because I just wanted to be alone and depressed.

The next week, I was walking to a class in the late

morning, and I noticed a table on the campus quad. It had a bunch of literature on it, mostly pamphlets, but a couple of Bibles, too. Then, I noticed the big wooden sign on an easel behind the table. I walked by as the smiling guy handed me an invitation to his Bible study, but I was in a rush so I just kept walking. Then, somebody in my brain delivered a message to my consciousness. "Wait, you fool! That wooden sign on the easel has the same design on it that the poster in the cafeteria did, and so does that invitation in your hand!!!" I stopped walking so abruptly that the person coming down the stairs behind me ran into my back. He said sorry, but I rudely ignored him and walked right back up to the table. The guy standing there smiled as I walked up, and I said none too kindly, "Where were you guys last Friday??? I went to the room and it was dark and nobody was there!"

He chuckled and said, "Hi, my name is _____."

I then realized what an ass I was being and said, "Oh, sorry, I'm Dan. Seriously, though, I went there and I was really bummed to find the room empty."

He explained that they had all been at a seminar the prior weekend in Fullerton, California. God had spoken through a man named Brother George. Over a thousand people were in attendance as the Spirit of God moved mightily and changed lives. That's why the room had been empty, but they would all be there that Friday.

Wow! The Spirit of God had moved ... and MIGHTILY! Amazed, I walked off to class, once again looking forward to Friday night. The week passed smoothly, and this time I knew my expectation was going to be fulfilled.

Friday *FINALLY* came. I arrived, and the room was not full. There were about ten people in a room that could seat four times that number. I walked in, with my memory full of proof texts that my eighteen-year-old self could use to argue my points and make sure this group had the right theology going for them (because, when you're eighteen you of course know what's best for everyone). What's a proof text? In this context, it is a Bible verse or verses that are memorized in order to be used as ammunition to prove that what one is saying is true. God had spoken to me about how things needed to be, and I was ready to teach them something. After all, just that week I had finished reading the entirety of the Bible from the first verse in Genesis straight through to the last verse in Revelation in the New International Version. How many other people could say that they had read the entire Bible from start to finish?

I had no idea what I was in for ... EVERYONE had read their Bibles ...

Most Bible studies in the group used a tool called Chapter Summary. Simply put, each week the Assembly would progress chapter by chapter through a book of the Bible. Each person in attendance was expected to have read, and studied the chapter beforehand in a specified format:

1. Outline—one would outline the chapter in a verse by verse breakdown.
2. Meaning—one would write a couple of paragraphs summarizing how the chapter "spoke" to them.
3. Memory Verse—one would memorize one verse from the chapter in order to help drive the message home.

As a kicker, anyone present could be called on by the leader to share what they had done. If you had not prepared, it was made clear through behavior and words that one had not met expectations (much more on this later). If one had prepared something, but the message one received from God was not in concert with the overall Assembly perspective, then one would be approached (possibly by more than one person) and they would address the error. If you nailed it, then it was made clear that you were on the right path. Psychologists will recognize the abusive manipulation being applied. Nail it ... reward. Miss it ... punishment. What follows is an example of a simple Chapter Summary Bible Study from one of the most beloved chapters in all of the Bible.

John Chapter 3:1-36 – King James Version

1 There was a man of the Pharisees, named Nicodemus, a ruler of the Jews: **2** The same came to Jesus by night, and said unto him, Rabbi, we know that thou art a teacher come from God: for no man can do these miracles that thou doest, except God be with him. **3** Jesus answered and said unto him, Verily, verily, I say unto thee, Except a man be born again, he cannot see the kingdom of God. **4** Nicodemus saith unto him, How can a man be born when he is old? can he enter the second time into his mother's womb, and be born? **5** Jesus answered, Verily, verily, I say unto thee, Except a man be born of water and *of* the Spirit, he cannot enter into the kingdom of God. **6** That which is born of the flesh is flesh; and that which is born of the Spirit is spirit. **7** Marvel not that I said unto thee, Ye must be born again. **8** The wind bloweth where it listeth, and thou hearest the sound thereof, but canst not tell whence it cometh, and whither it goeth: so is every one that is born of the Spirit. **9** Nicodemus answered and said unto him, How can these things be? **10** Jesus answered and said unto him, Art thou a master of Israel, and knowest not these things? **11** Verily, verily, I say unto thee, We speak that we do know, and testify that we have seen; and ye receive not our witness. **12** If I have told you earthly things, and ye believe not, how shall ye believe, if I tell you *of* heavenly things? **13** And no man hath ascended up to heaven, but he that came down from heaven, *even* the Son of man which is in heaven. **14** And as Moses lifted up the serpent in the wilderness, even so must the Son of man be lifted up: **15** That whosoever believeth in him should not perish, but have eternal life. **16** For God so loved the world, that he gave his only begotten Son, that whosoever believeth in him should not perish, but have everlasting life. **17** For God sent not his Son into the world to condemn the world; but that the world through him might be saved. **18** He that believeth on him is not condemned: but he that believeth not is condemned already, because he hath not believed in the name of the only begotten Son of God. **19** And this is the condemnation, that light is come into the world, and men loved darkness rather than light, because their deeds were evil. **20** For every one that doeth evil hateth the light, neither cometh to the light, lest his deeds should be reproved. **21** But he that doeth truth cometh to the light, that his deeds may be made manifest, that they are wrought in God. **22** After these things came Jesus and his disciples into the land of Judaea; and there he tarried with them, and baptized. **23** And John also was baptizing in Aenon near to Salim, because there was much water there: and they came, and were baptized. **24** For John was not yet cast into prison. **25** Then there arose a question between *some* of John's disciples and the Jews about purifying. **26** And they came unto John, and said unto him, Rabbi, he that was with thee beyond Jordan, to whom thou barest witness, behold, the same baptizeth, and all *men* come to him. **27** John answered and said, A man can receive nothing, except it be given him from heaven. **28** Ye yourselves bear me witness, that I said, I am not the Christ, but that I am sent before him. **29** He that hath the bride is the bridegroom: but the friend of the bridegroom, which standeth and heareth him, rejoiceth greatly because of the bridegroom's voice: this my joy therefore is fulfilled. **30** He must increase, but I *must* decrease. **31** He that cometh from above is above all: he that is of the earth is earthly, and speaketh of the earth: he that cometh from heaven is above all. **32** And what he hath seen and heard, that he testifieth; and no man receiveth his testimony. **33** He that hath received his testimony hath set to his seal that God is true. **34** For he whom God hath sent speaketh the words of God: for God giveth not the Spirit by measure *unto him*. **35** The Father loveth the Son, and hath given all things into his hand. **36** He that believeth on the Son hath everlasting life: and he that believeth not the Son shall not see life; but the wrath of God abideth on him.

Example Chapter Summary
Part 1 – Verse by Verse Outline
1–8 A Matter of Birth
9–21 God so Loved the World
22–36 He Must Increase and I Must Decrease

Part 2 – What Does the Chapter Mean to Me?
Nicodemus did not understand what it means to be born again. We are all born spiritually dead, and it is Christ that makes us alive when we receive him. Receiving him and being made spiritually alive is being born again. Once you are born again, then you need to walk in light. If I truly love light, then my deeds will be good and all men will see that they are good. Those who love darkness will see and hate it because they do not love light. One way that I know I am walking in the Spirit is that the world (including

worldly Christians) hates me, but true believers love me and what I do. Finally, I must decrease. In all things people need to see Christ. I can get in the way of that, so I need to be humble and decrease. As I decrease, He will increase and the Spirit will be able to work.

Part 3 – Memory Verse
30 He must increase, but I *must* decrease.

Wait … I wrote that? Wow …
Every Friday that classes were in session, for those involved with the college ministry, as well as every Thursday at the local meeting hall for everyone in the local Assembly, we would all be expected to do our chapter summaries. We could be in the Old or New Testaments. We could be told that we would march through any book (genealogies and all) and that God wanted us to be good stewards of what He had given us. We all needed to be prepared each week. There were very few reasons that one could have for not being at a meeting, and if you came there were even fewer reasons to excuse not being ready with something to share.

That Friday, as I mentioned, the leader went through an outline of the entire book we were going to be studying that year (I can't at this point remember what book it was, but I think it was the Gospel of John). Rather than doing a verse outline, he did a chapter outline. He did a book meaning. He did a memory verse intended to communicate the meaning of the entire book. After the study, I went up and talked to him on a wide range of topics from the Bible. What did he believe about this that and the other thing? What did they teach? Where did they find it in the Bible? I gave him the full rundown, and he also gave it back to me. Afterwards, we all went out to a local coffee shop and talked about more Bible topics. One guy in particular took an interest in my spiritual development. I didn't know at the time, but the leader had suggested that he disciple me. Hereafter I'll refer to him as "Shepherd." I was so impressed by everyone's zeal for holiness and righteousness. God was just about the only thing they could talk about!

This was it! This was the group I wanted to be in. Every person there seemed to be serious about God. All of them were well versed in the Bible and ready to share what they knew with anyone at any time. THESE WERE CHRISTIANS!!!!! I thought that my days of struggling alone for righteousness were over, for here was a group of people that would help me to be a new man and live a different life! I was invited to join them for their Sunday afternoon Bible study. I thought they just worshipped in the afternoon rather than the morning, but I was wrong. I went to the local Presbyterian Church in the morning. In the Assembly, you weren't invited to Sunday worship until they were sure you were a serious Christian. Sunday morning was not a time for visitors. It was a time for the Lord's chosen people. That's why I had no idea they even worshipped on Sunday morning.

As I sat there that Sunday afternoon next to Shepherd and talked, I noticed that there were families and that the children were all present in the meeting. There appeared to be no separate Sunday School or anything of that nature. There were mats on the floor for the children to sleep on or play quietly. Everyone was together, children and all, and there seemed to be an expectation and excitement about the coming Bible study. As we began, the first shock I got was the singing. When we stood to sing, there were no instruments of any kind. The leader in front just sang, and we all followed along. Even more shocking than the lack of instruments was *how* they sang. Everyone just *belted* it out. Good voice, bad voice, whatever ... they all shook the rooftops. I'm sure people in neighboring counties could hear it all. Once again, these people had to love God. Look at the way they just poured themselves into it with no reservation. After the singing, there were three preachers. The first shared a gospel message intended to convert any unbelieving visitors. The second shared a twenty-minute word of encouragement on a general Bible topic of their choice. Finally, the main event was a long message from a predetermined book of the Bible that they studied together, but not in Chapter Summary format. The preacher used Chapter Summary format to share his message, but nobody else was expected to be called upon. Everyone in the room had notebooks out. Everyone was taking notes. Everyone was AMEN-ing and PRAISE THE LORD-ing at various points that they found either encouraging or challenging. I also noticed that for every open Bible I saw, there were notes written in people's margins. They all took this very seriously.

The men were all dressed in nice shirts and ties. The women were all dressed in clothing that showed virtually nothing of their bodies ... and virtually no makeup to be seen anywhere. All of the women also wore coverings over their heads during the meeting (not at all times, just during the meeting). Every other youth group or Bible study group I had been to in my life had the typical characters. You know, "studly guy" and "cleavage girl" and

"I'm too cool for Sunday School jock" and "OMG Becky did you see *that*" girl. The typical immature mix consisting of a select few people who were serious about things, and the rest of the people who were just there for other reasons. Not with this group. Every single person in that room was serious about what they were doing.

This is part of how they reeled me in. Everyone was so intent on being righteous and holy. Everything they did seemed to be geared for maximal purity. No other Christian group I had ever encountered was so fixed upon making sure that every last thought, word, and deed was focused on pleasing God. It seemed that every last person in the group wanted nothing more than to make God proud. THIS was what I wanted!

Afterwards, Shepherd asked me what I thought of the messages. I told him what had impressed me and asked some questions. We then spoke to a number of other people there, including the other two leaders whom I had not met at the campus Bible study. In the Assembly, there was always more than one leader at a local gathering. This, they said, was for accountability. They were all men. They worked together. Women were strictly forbidden from any and all leadership positions, and were never allowed to preach. Not only that, but as I mentioned, the group also strictly adhered to a requirement that all women wear head coverings at prayer and worship meetings. At first, I did not like this part ... I considered it more than a little sexist, actually. However, look at the zealous pursuit of righteousness here! I decided to stick around and see what they would say about it.

Before I left, Shepherd asked me if I wanted to go through the "four anchors" with him. This was a discipleship tool used by the Assembly. The four anchors of the faith were fellowship, worship, the Word, and prayer. These four things would keep a believer rooted and grounded in the faith. But that's not all! These four things were to be practiced individually and as a group. All four things were to be pursued with utter zeal both individually and at group meetings. Only then would you be rooted in holiness such that you could walk with Jesus well and be pleasing to him.

Shepherd and I began meeting weekly, going through the Bible and studying each of these four things, and I continued attending the Thursday, Friday, and Sunday afternoon meetings as well. I was taught that everyone else in the world ... family, friends, even other Christians, were to be treated with suspicion. Each one could be used by Satan to discourage and stumble me. Each one could prove to be the thing that would rob me of an inheritance. What is an inheritance? Well, to use the archetype from the Old Testament, there were Christians that would overcome and enter the Promised Land. Then there were others who did not overcome and perished in the wilderness, never having reached the Promised Land. They were saved just like the people of old had been saved by passing through the Red Sea, and would not go to Hell, but they would not inherit the kingdom. They would live on the New Earth, but the overcomers would live in the Heavenly City ... the New Jerusalem. This is where I wanted to be. This is where ALL of these people wanted to be. This is how I was ensnared. The sincere desire of all of these people, combined with the apparent focus on God's holiness, and the ardently targeted teaching. That is what I wanted. I would give my all to get it. I told Shepherd that

I was all in and I wanted to devote my life to this.

Wait, what do you mean you don't date?

That revelation stopped me in my tracks for a second. No dating allowed. A single brother was never to go anywhere alone with a single sister unless they were out preaching the gospel (witnessing), having been assigned to a group together by the witnessing leader. In fact, single brothers were not allowed into the homes of single sisters (even in groups) unless accompanied by a married couple. There was rigid enforcement of this rule. There was literally the fear that if a single man and woman would be alone in a home together, their passion would flare up and sexual immorality would immediately and uncontrollably ensue. It was as if leadership believed that every single (meaning unmarried) man and woman on earth is just wandering around in a permanent state of arousal waiting to jump on every unsuspecting member of the opposite sex possible. Even groups of single people were not to be found in a home together ... as if all of us were constantly thinking about crazy orgies or some other nonsense. If a brother so much as laid a hand on a sister, other than a handshake, there was a talking-to involved. Merely sitting in a chair next to the same sister two meetings in a row might result in a talking-to. Some Assembly leaders took it so far as to teach that if an engaged couple (mind you, engaged and on the way to marriage) was to kiss, this was considered a sin. Kissing your fiancé, for some in the group, was a sin of immorality and an open door for Satan to tempt you into folly. You could hold hands, or hug, but kissing prior to the wedding day was just taking things too far for these leaders. Looking back, I'm actually surprised that they didn't enforce separate seating in public gatherings for men and women like many conservative religions do.

Where the core leader of the group, Brother George, had gotten the idea that people are just perverts waiting to pounce on innocent victims became quite clear later on.

As I considered this newly acquired knowledge about dating, several things whirled through my mind. How would I get married? How did one learn the dos and don'ts of a relationship? How would you determine if someone was right for you? "Trust the Lord and He will provide," was the mantra. This is something I would hear all too often about all too many things. Just trust the will of God. Rational thinking, serious planning, and other such things were often set aside as we "Trusted the Lord" for things great and small.

How far did this "just trust the Lord" thinking go for some? One sister had a betta fish tank. It was one of those that had a piece of clear media between the two fishes. They could display at each other, nip at the clear glass/plastic, do their rituals, and then go their separate ways. She decided she would "trust the Lord" for them. She prayed that they would be friends, removed the separating media, and watched in horror. The betta fish immediately turned on each other and tore each other to pieces. "They are sinning!" cried the sister. No, they are being betta fish. "Trusting the Lord" in such ridiculous ways was common. The brother who refused to save for retirement because he "trusted the Lord" to provide for him and his wife in their elder years. The brother who refused to study because he "trusted the Lord" to provide for his exams. Finally, just "trust the Lord" and take zero family planning into consideration whatsoever. Just keep pumping out the kids, no consideration of whether it was in your budget, and "God will provide." "Just trust the Lord" was taken way too far for a good many people in the group.

For now, suffice it to say that I would not be dating anyone or experiencing any romance at all for a very long time. One sister would actually organize events for single women that she called "Rotic" events. What was a "Rotic"? Well, she explained that it was romantic without the man. Ro-tic. Lighted candles, soft music, nice ambiance ... no men. Just women. People took the "no dating" rule very seriously.

In addition, every time I expressed any interest at all in someone, the leadership was quick to quash it, saying that they were my "sister" and I needed to think about things that way. Wait, look at this person as if they are actually my sister? [vomits in mouth] That definitely removes any romantic interest. Finally, any consideration of a serious relationship with someone outside the Assembly, even from another evangelical church, was frowned upon. During my nearly ten years in the group, I knew some people who married outside the Assembly, and those individuals definitely knew that their behavior was met with disapproval.

As concerns flooded my mind about this "no dating" standard, however, something else popped into my head. As an eighteen-year-old man, sexual desire was a huge part of my life. One of the reasons I had "failed" in resisting "sexual temptation" in the past was the fact that I *had* dated. I *had* kissed girlfriends. I *had* explored my sexuality (although I had never experienced intercourse). The more I thought about it, I considered the rule of forced "no dating" actually a good thing. I wouldn't fall into sexual sin for one clear reason ... by never dating and never being alone with a member of the opposite sex, I would never have *opportunity* to give in to sexual temptation. Strangely, therefore, the "no dating" standard actually helped the cult to seal the deal and secure my commitment. Remember, I believed that the avalanche in March 1995 was a warning from God. Shape up, or else. I was absolutely convinced at this point that the Assembly culture would allow me to be protected from God's judgment by keeping me from sin. I would finally be sexually pure because I would simply never have any opportunity to fall into sin ... at least with another person.

On my own in a shower? Yeah, been there done that.

In general, this was a way the Assembly was structured about everything. You would be pure because every facet of your life would be so rigidly bound by rules, and scrupulously observed by leadership, that you would be *kept* from sin through group control of both your actions and your thinking.

Other Christians I had met had various reactions to learning which group I had become involved in. Some came right out and warned me that I had become involved in a cult. Others were more diplomatic about it and said the group was "problematic." Why did I dismiss the concerns not only of my parents, my old friends, professors ... and even other Christians? Simple. It was the zeal for holiness that seemed to permeate every single individual and every single fabric of Assembly culture. Even though direct warnings that I was getting involved with a cult were coming in, I shrugged it all off because I was actually remaining "pure" in this environment.

Nothing, at this point, would dissuade me from getting further involved.

Shepherd and I continued through our discipleship meetings. As I mentioned, I had just finished reading the Bible from start to finish, and I immediately went right back to Genesis and began the process again. I bought a Cambridge Press King James Bible. I still have it. I'm actually reading it through again as I create this manuscript. There is something about the smell of the leather of that Bible that is magical to me. Also, there is something about the language of the King James. Despite the archaic English, it is just beautiful. Despite all of the problems in the translation, and the politics woven into it, it is my favorite. Poetry, drama, passion. Everything seems to be emphasized in this translation of the scripture. For the second time, I began reading the Bible straight through from the beginning of Genesis to the end of Revelation. When I finished it in the King James early the next year, I went right back to Genesis and started again in the same translation.

Side note ... as of today, I've read the Bible from start straight through to finish eight times. My current rereading of the King James is therefore my ninth time reading the entirety of the Bible. Some of my favorite books of the Bible, like the Gospel of John, I honestly don't know how many times I've read.

Immediately, the Assembly leadership began teaching in a very targeted way as I was discipled. When I was saved, they said with strong emphasis, God called me out of the world and into his light. Like the ancient Israelites being called out of Egypt to forge their own theocratic nation, I was called out of the world to live my life almost exclusively in the presence of other believers ... in particular, Assembly believers. Out of Egypt, through the wilderness, and into the Promised Land! The story of the Exodus was a metaphor for the Christian life. God saved you when he delivered you from Egypt through the Red Sea. He was taking you to the Promised Land. The Promised Land was not Heaven, but "victorious Christian living" while still here on Earth. The wandering in the wilderness is what a Christian goes through prior to achieving that "life of victory." So, you see, even other believers by and large were worldly and needed to be avoided. The vast majority of Christians on Earth, it was taught, were wandering in the wilderness like the ancient Israelites. They had been delivered from Egypt (salvation), but they had not achieved the life of victory (conquering Israel) and were therefore wandering in the wilderness. The conclusion was that the only true place I could be confident that I would be "out of the world" was in the Assembly where we had received a special revelation and possessed special "light" that other Christians lacked. I concluded that to truly be separated from the world it was critically important that I sever ties with "worldly" friends, "worldly" Christians ... even family.

I could be a "witness" to them through my separation.

I recall conversations about this very clearly. "Dan," said the leaders, "think about your struggles as a teenager. If you hadn't been around people tempting you to sin, would you have done it? It's critical to remove people from your life that Satan could use as a stumbling block." This, they argued, was how the world could bring me back down. It wasn't, however, just nonbelievers that could lead me astray. Other Christians would also tempt me. They watched certain "defiling" movies, and entertained impure things that we simply did not in the Assembly (heck, nobody even had a TV ... nothing of perceived worldliness was allowed). I could be brought down by other believers as well. We were to be a shining city on a hill, our walls of purity protecting us from the dangers of the world without. Venturing out of that holy city for school, employment, etc. was necessary to survive and therefore had to be done, but we would always have a refuge to return to where the light of the Holy Spirit held sway and we could be protected from the evils without the walls. The Bible talks about this in terms of being "in the world, but not *of* the world."

This is how I was ensnared ... and the shocking thing is, as most people who have come out of cults will tell you, I began actively helping them to further ensnare me not even realizing what I was doing.

In the coming months, I would cut off from my life the people I had only just met in the dorms. I would cut off from my life old friends from high school. While it is normal for the majority of one's high school friends to pass from one's life with time, I would cast particularly harsh judgment on one of my old high school friends and we parted on very bad terms. Deep regret sat heavily on my shoulders for many years about this, but I am happy to say that today we are friends once again.

Steve, thanks for understanding.

I isolated myself entirely, such that the only people I had any real relation to in the world were my Assembly brothers and sisters and my immediate family. However, I even began distancing myself from that same family as well. Most college students spend holiday breaks at home with family (unless they go on some road trip with friends). Me? I would spend perhaps a week or two at home during Christmas break, and the same during the summer. My parents lamented the fact that I was rarely home. I lived, ate, slept, and breathed Assembly living and this is the way the leadership wanted it. Going home, you see, was an opportunity for Satan to come in with temptations and lead one astray.

Going to class and work were an unavoidable and necessary part of life, so exposure to "the world" there was something I would have to pray about and work to remain faithful in. I would be in classes or work environments with men and women, homosexual, trans ... every part of the rainbow that is expression of human identity. However, I would preach to these people. I would be a witness of what it means to be holy. I would stand up for biblical principles in classes and speak out against abortion, evolution, or other topics if they came up in classes. Also, since I was not in a coed dorm building, I didn't need to make any changes to my living arrangements. There were cases of individuals in coed dorms where they were "strongly encouraged" to convince the school to allow them to move to another dorm building based on religious reasons.

An example of how this would work is something like a study group. If I was assigned to some team effort by a professor, I would adamantly insist that all such meetings with that assigned group were to be held in public places like a coffee shop or library. I would stubbornly refuse any such meetings at an individual's home. Remember, unmarried individuals were never to be alone in private, even in groups. So, meeting in public was a way I could show the world that I was a pure Christian. Allegations that I was being romantic with someone or in any other way impure would be very difficult to make since I was always in public with members of the opposite gender.

Another example with regard to employment is a refusal to ever work on a Sunday. I had a retail job, as the reader may recall, and that store was open on Sundays. However, I was to explain to the owner that I needed a religious exemption so I could worship. Since the owner of That Candle Store was Christian, this was an easy sell at that job which lasted for the first two years of my college tenure. Other examples of how to remain pure at work were things like never being alone in the back of the store with a member of the opposite gender, and (as my career progressed later) never traveling alone with a member of the opposite gender. Once again, if I was never in a situation where I was alone with a member of the opposite gender then there could never be any doubt with regard to my Christian purity.

I recall one Saturday perhaps a month after school had started during my freshman year. There was a "fellowship" (it's really just a fancy word for getting together socially) at one of the leader's homes. It was a BBQ, and the home had a view of the ocean. That day in the fall, as many are, was clear and warm. Everyone from the local Assembly was there. I had, at that point, isolated myself so completely from everyone else I could possibly know in Humboldt County that I was struggling with deep loneliness. As I drove away at the end of that event, I actually cried. Why did I need to be so alone? Why was the world such a dark and terrifying place where Satan might ambush me around any corner? Why did I only see these people a few days out of the week? Shepherd called me that night and invited me to worship the next morning. This would be my first time attending their worship service, and I was informed that there was the expectation of a suits and ties level of formality. I recall thinking, "Wait, you guys have worship in the morning???" I thought their afternoon meeting was it for them on Sundays. I had a nice suit that was a graduation gift from my folks, but that was it.

Shepherd informed me that not only did they meet on Sunday mornings *and* afternoons (all day for God, they called it), but there were lots of other meetings that I was invited to as well. Tuesday prayer meeting, I was already attending Thursday community Bible study and Friday campus Bible study, and Saturday morning (by morning, I mean *early* morning) "tape ministry" where we listened to recordings of the founder of the group preaching long sermons. How long? I mean these were generally two-hour messages ... and they were very dry. He thought he was the best preacher ever to walk the earth, but the reality was quite different. Since I was now deemed serious enough to be fully involved in every meeting, there would only be two nights per week that I would have to be alone! I could be surrounded in my city on the hill almost constantly, and since Shepherd and I generally met on Wednesdays, I was spending nearly every day of the week immersed in the Assembly culture.

I had, it seemed, been deemed worthy to be fully involved in everything they did.

Any psychologist reading this is probably jumping up and down screaming at this point, because they understand *exactly* what the intent of all of this was.

Separate me from everyone else that could possibly influence me, drive into my naïve and idealistic thinking the idea that the Assembly was the one source in all the world for truth and real happiness, and truly deep levels of psychological control would be achieved. The vast majority of those in the Assembly would not call it control. Huge amounts of mental gymnastics were constantly performed to use semantics in redefining things throughout life. They called it accountability. Once I was separated, then I was ready to move up the ladder and get serious. I had no other emotional support that I trusted (again, even my parents were put on the "naughty" list), and if I left the Assembly, I would be completely alone ... again. Remember my struggles with loneliness that I just discussed? The reality that leaving would render me more alone than ever before since I had cut off everyone I knew, and done so in a manner that was both condescending and offensive, created an empty feeling of desperation. Leaving would mean *utter* loneliness on a level I could scarcely imagine. Besides, I wanted to serve and please God. Where else could I do that as well as in the Assembly where quite literally everyone involved talked about almost nothing else every time we were together? Everything was "the Lord" this and "Jesus" that and "He is so good to me about _____" other thing. Never had I encountered people that literally could not stop talking about God. Every conversation had to come back to him. I can vividly remember feeling guilty when a conversation took place where the almighty dictator never came up. If I had a conversation on any topic that I could not somehow tie back to God, I felt as if I had failed Him somehow.

    The fall semester continued to progress. Classes and

work continued to be challenging on some levels. I had put in place the aforementioned standards for maintaining my Christian purity, but all around me were relationships with happy young couples exploring their romantic identities, challenges to my views on LGBTQ+ issues, and science classes that forced me to face "Bible or science fact" types of worldview choices. Also, even though I was in a dorm suite that was not coed, the guys were always having parties with alcohol, drugs, and women. For whatever reason, I've never been a fan of such parties, so the dorm was more of a frustration than a problem of temptation. However, I lost a lot of sleep to loud music and drunken parties in and around my dorm suite. I had signed an agreement for an alcohol-free dorm suite, but that was *not* what was delivered. I loathed my dorm life.

The rains of the Pacific Northwest began to fall (little did I know that it would rain almost without stop from mid-October to late April). The holiday season approached. I was about to learn something else shocking that would impact my worldview. Christmas and Easter were pagan holidays ... and Halloween was just Satanic worship of demons. Actually, the part about Christmas and Easter is true. These were pagan holidays many long years ago. There are in fact people that still celebrate the pagan rituals, many of them concentrated in places like Humboldt County. The Catholic Church co-opted these pagan holidays into Christendom during the late third and early fourth centuries CE (Common Era). The Assembly taught that buying Christmas presents and participating in Easter was to honor paganism, and we did not believe in celebrating those holidays. Many members would take offense if someone said "bless you" after a sneeze. My first real challenge was, therefore, during the Christmas break that year. I actually did spend the entire four-week break at my parents' house. It would be the last long break I would ever spend at my parents' home. I bought everyone Christmas presents (incurring the judgment of Assembly leadership in the process) and spent more than a little bit of time skiing at Mammoth.

I was also "tempted" during my time away, but did not fall to the "temptations."

When I came back to Arcata, however, I was glad to return to my city on the hill. I was once again secure in those walls of Christian purity and safe from the dangers of the world. Based on what I heard from others in the Assembly when I returned, and based on being "tempted" at home, I decided that was it. I would no longer spend more than a week or two at a time away from the Assembly.

My parents were very hurt when I told them I couldn't maintain purity in my spiritual life at their house.

Late January each year there was a conference for college students. It was called the Campus Conference. There were regional meetings for college students around the nation. Ours was held that year in a youth hostel north of San Francisco, but south of Bodega Bay. I had an amazing time. Preachers from the Fullerton Assembly were there, one of the founder's sons and another preacher unrelated to the founder. Both of them really amazed me at that time. This was my first encounter with people from the group that were not from Arcata. All of them had the same perspective the Arcata group did. God first. Everything else second. The ultimate HE was all we talked about. We had a rousing game of mud football out in the rain, and all in all it was a great weekend. I was encouraged that there were others around the country (and world) that shared our vision. Our city on the hill was not the only one ... there were others we were connected to.

Upon returning from that event, classes started up and we got back at it with the preaching. During the spring semester of my first year, there was a campus camping trip. We went to Patrick's Point State Park. It was a simple overnight camping trip with all of the usual camping activities, plus Bible discussion and prayer times mixed in. I recall sitting on the bluffs watching waves crashing in on the rocks, sending foamy white water high into the air. Seals and sea lions played in the surf and barked. The forests marched right down to the cliff's edge, with meadows mixed in. This trip taught me that we would spend recreation time together (and outdoor recreation at that), and even that recreation would be centered on some Bible activity or other. I was confident, therefore, that my love of the outdoors was something I could continue to enjoy, albeit now in a way entirely focused on the Lord. We would regularly have little events where we would go out to a local beach for games, BBQ, or just walking. This *was* about building relationships and community, but it was never just to have a good time or relax. There was always some greater lesson or Bible study worked into it. Our whole lives, therefore, revolved unceasingly around study of scripture, even in leisure activities. Also, when we did go out to class or work, we always had a safe place to come back to.

They were the city on the hill. The only safe refuge. Even their leisure activities were centered around the

Most High. At that time in my life, all I wanted was to please God, and I wanted every single aspect of my life to be pleasing in His most holy sight. So far as I could tell, everyone else in the group wanted the exact same thing. *This* was the place where I would learn *true* holiness. This was the place where I would avoid the snares of the devil. This was the place where my life would please God to the fullest extent possible.

That was it. They got me. I was wholly ensnared by the group by the end of my first year of college. That summer (1996) I would have some doubts, but they would all fade away the more I immersed myself. I truly believed that this was the only place I could live a holy and righteous life pleasing to God in every way. I truly believed that every environment outside the group was a place where the Enemy could tempt and distract me from the pursuit of true holiness. I was an Assembly man, and every single decision I made in college from that point forward would deepen my commitment and my fanaticism.

Once again, however, I still had no idea what I was getting myself into.

Chapter Three
Daily Assembly Life

The degree to which a person's life was affected by the Assembly was entirely proportional to one's devotion to the group. Yes, that is a no-brainer. For someone who attended some meetings but didn't go to social events and didn't live in one of the training homes, they might appreciate the Bible study and get some insight from what was taught. Things like "no dating" and other such rules would seem like silly annoyances that distracted from the teaching, rather than practices that caused severe emotional/psychological damage. What follows is what my daily Assembly life was like, including living in one of the communal living situations that they called biblical training homes.

Towards the end of my freshman year of college (spring 1996), I received two invitations. One, to be a counselor on the five-week Teen Team. Two, to move into a brothers home upon my return to Arcata after the conclusion of the summer team. The first was a missionary training team for teens in the Assembly. Most of the counselors were college-aged men and women brought along to help shepherd the teens through the tough questions and experiences of adolescence. It would be four weeks of evangelism as a group combined with direct training from the founder of the cult in Fullerton and surrounding cities, followed by a week at Mammoth, just forty-five minutes from my hometown. I jumped on it at the first opportunity, even though I barely had the cash to do it (more on finances later).

Memorial Day weekend every year there was a regional Assembly conference called the Northwest Conference. It included groups from as far south as San Luis Obispo, California, and as far north as Seattle, Washington. Unlike the Campus Conference, which was limited to college students, this was open to families and people of all ages in the Assembly. The preachers were both sons of the founder. I had met one of his sons, Tim, before. However, it was my first introduction to his other son, David, from San Luis Obispo. Suffice it to say, unlike his brother Tim, David was not a warm or charismatic person. He struck me as an authoritarian, but I wrote off my first impression at the time. In addition to that, I just didn't get a good vibe regarding his dynamic with his wife and children. Something struck me as off about the whole situation.

David will play a significant role later on.

That year the Northwest Conference was held in the Oregon Cascades northeast of Klamath Falls, Oregon. I decided to attend on my way home to visit with my folks after the spring semester had ended. It wasn't really on the way at all, but I wanted the experience. The conference was about a week after the end of the spring semester, so I spent a few days staying at one of the leading brothers homes. There was normally a monetary cost for individuals to attend this, but given my low-income college self, one of the leaders in Arcata paid my fee that year. It was a great weekend. I'd never been to that area of Oregon before, so the environment really amazed me. One of the massive stratovolcanoes that make the Cascades what they are was just a few miles west of the site. People played outdoor games, sat and looked at stars, walked in the woods ... all while discussing God and the Bible. The trip further solidified my commitment to the group and introduced me to more members from faraway places. This confirmed, in my mind, that I could move on in life and serve in a city on a hill in another location should I move away from Arcata at some point in the future.

After the conference, I was only at home with my family for two weeks before the Teen Team started in late June, and they were really disappointed that I would be leaving so quickly. My family, both immediate and extended, as well as old friends, expressed no small amount of concern with regard to how this religious group was coming to dominate every single decision I made and every single aspect of my life. My folks were very concerned that I would be moving into a brothers home upon returning to Humboldt State in the fall of 1996. Also, I missed the high school graduation of a dear childhood friend because of the Team (sorry, Kenny).

The Teen Team involved a summer school program where the founder of the cult led us chapter by chapter through a book of the Bible. They were two-hour class sessions, four days per week, and we went through the book of 1 Corinthians. In addition to that, we went to all of the local Assembly meetings, plus outreach events where we went street preaching, plus specific Teen Team meetings. Oh ... we went to the beach, too. Men could basically wear whatever they wanted for swimming, but there was a strict dress code for sisters. One-piece bathing suits *plus* shorts were required. Once again, women were controlled very closely lest the men fall to animal temptation and go crazy (or something). What did they think would happen anyway? Would we just tackle a bikini-clad sister on the spot? There were other women at the beach in bikinis and we weren't tackling them to the ground. Misogyny was rampant in this cult, as it is in many Christian churches.

It was a very busy summer, and that is an understatement.

By the time the relaxation week in Mammoth came, I was exhausted. However, I was really happy to spend that week so close to where I grew up. If the reader has never been to Mammoth Lakes, California, I can't recommend it strongly enough at any season of the year. The winter skiing is simply the best California has to offer, and the summer hiking, fishing, mountain biking, and other outdoor adventure opportunities are amazing. We hiked, we played sports, we swam in the chilled snowmelt of mountain lakes and rivers, and we enjoyed the myriad stars that appeared in mountain skies. Overall, it was a good summer, and the Teen Team further cemented my commitment to the group. It was this experience that completely erased the doubts I mentioned earlier.

The second invitation to move into a brothers home in Arcata when I returned from summer was something else I jumped on. Since I would be living with the family of one of the leaders *and* there would be other unmarried men as my roommates, this would eliminate the feeling of loneliness that had plagued me during my entire first year of college. Which home it would be was undecided, but I would pray and so would the leaders back in Humboldt. They would let me know when the time came. Once again, I would just need to trust the Lord.

No planning.

No rational thought about best fit.

Just pray and trust God to speak and lead.

After the Teen Team, I was only at home for another two weeks before returning to Arcata. My family was devastated that after my first year of college I only spent a total of four weeks at home during the summer of 1996. My cousins had all returned to their homes for the majority of the summer to work and spend time with family. I ran off as fast as I could to avoid the temptation of the Adversary. Remember … I wanted to please God, and any time spent away from the group was additional time given to Satan to temp me. As a result, while trips to see family were not discouraged in principle, long trips where one would be away for an extended period were absolutely frowned upon. "Brother, the Lord called you *here*, not there. Don't you think you should be spending your time laboring for Him in the locality to which God has called you rather than spending extended leisure time somewhere else? Did Jesus ever take a vacation?" Literally, these were some of the arguments used. "Did Jesus ever take a vacation?" [smacks forehead] To a naïve and highly idealistic young adult (especially one whose life goal was ostensibly to please God in every way), these were convincing words indeed.

Here, I must once again stress that this dear family, in whose home I lived for nearly five years, has repented of any and all harm they caused to the fullest degree that is reasonable and possible. I am on good terms with them today and on the rare occasions where we communicate, it is always positive.

When I think about it, I actually miss them.

Upon my return to Arcata, I did move into one of the leader's homes. They had five boys. As an aside, when I moved out five years later, I asked their youngest boy (he would be going to kindergarten that fall) if he could remember a time when I did not live with them. He looked sad, and shook his head "no." To him, there was never a time that I was not a part of his home, so my departure was a major change in his young little world. When I moved in, there were two other brothers living in the home with the family. I started working for the painting business that the head of the home ran for a couple of weeks until my That Candle Store job started. It was August 1996 and I had left the Eastern High Sierra on a 90-degree summer day to arrive in fifty-degree McKinleyville, California. Crystal clear deep blue mountain skies exchanged for a gray fog that seemed to be melting itself onto everything in a frigid and steady drip. What had happened to summer? I knew it could be foggy and cold in the Pacific Northwest, but 50 degrees in August ... really???

Depression immediately and *powerfully* seized hold of me.

A wet blanket (much like the dripping fog layer over the entire coastal part of the county) weighed me down at all times as I struggled with the emotion. However, I believed this was my cross to bear and that I was doing the will of God. This was pleasing to Him. One of the other brothers who worked for the painting business during the summers saw that I was not doing well and did his best to be encouraging and supportive.

He and I would end up becoming very good friends in the group, although we have drifted apart since it collapsed.

As the days passed, I got accustomed to being in damp and cold Humboldt County when everything inside me was screaming for real summer weather. The day in and day out of Assembly home life, working, Assembly meetings, rinse repeat began to take on some normalcy. Also, there were a number of events that raised my morale pretty strongly. There were BBQs, trips inland to local rivers where it was actually still warm and the swimming was good, lots of encouragement in the form of biblical preaching, and to cap it all off there was the Assembly camping trip before the fall semester began. Most of the members of the Arcata Assembly considered this a highlight of the year. Once again, I was able to go out and explore the outdoors along rivers running through coastal redwoods.

My normal day in the Assembly was something like this:

- 5:30-6 a.m.: wake up/shower time
- 6-7 a.m.: private morning prayer and Bible study time
- 7-7:30 a.m.: breakfast with the whole home
    - Meals were eaten together almost every day of the week when one lived in a home, and each brother living there was assigned to prepare one breakfast and one dinner every week.
- 7:30 a.m.: leave for school/work, depending on the day and whether or not the semester was in session

- 8 a.m.–approximately 4:30 p.m.: work/ school/ campus gospel preaching
- 4:30–6 p.m.: return home to prepare for and have house dinner
- 6–7 p.m.: prep for evening meeting if there was one, study for classes if no meeting
- 7–9 p.m.: evening meeting if there was one, study for classes if no meeting
- 9 p.m.: daily chores that needed to be done each evening
- 9:30–10 p.m.: evening private prayer and Bible study time
    - If you lived in a home, you would often pray with the other unmarried people living with the family during this time slot.
- Rinse/repeat the next day, all under the supervision of the leader one lived with who would monitor your activities and rebuke or praise where appropriate.

Criticism was far more common than praise when it came to anything. We submitted sermons to the leader for his review (brothers, in particular those in training homes, were expected to be ready to preach a sermon at every prayer meeting and worship time), he reviewed all of our chores, he monitored how we spent our time, monitored how we prepared meals ... everything.

I remember being criticized for things like leaving a single hair on the base of the toilet during a cleaning, being five minutes late with dinner on the night I was cooking, mowing the lawn in such a way that it had slightly uneven rows or furrows in the grass ... nothing was off-limits. Everything was an indication of how serious we were about our commitment to God. That single hair you left on the toilet? That was an indication that you were not diligent about eliminating every flaw in your walk with Jesus. That five minutes you were late with dinner? That was an indication that you lacked the faithfulness to keep your commitments with exactitude. Those furrows you left in the lawn? That was an indication of your inconsistent application of the Word of God in your life.

You see, in Luke 16:10 (New International Version) Jesus said, "Whoever can be trusted with very little can also be trusted with much, and whoever is dishonest with very little will also be dishonest with much." Even in these little household chores, if you could not be faithful then it was an indication that you would be faithless with greater responsibilities. So, I always found myself trying to do everything perfectly, and since I am an imperfect, flawed human being, I was always failing to meet that perfect standard. This kept me feeling that I needed Jesus's mercy for everything. That I needed the Assembly life and protection to keep me. That I needed to keep myself from outside influences such that I would be more faithful to the little things. After all, hadn't Jesus himself said in Luke that the little things were important markers of the quality of our spiritual lives? I was continually driven by guilt and a perceived need for mercy, and it could be something as minor as leaving a single hair on the base of a toilet that would drive me to my knees in tearful repentance for my faithlessness.

This standard of perfection applied to our interactions with the regular world as well. Recall from the prior chapter that I had methods for managing my involvement with outsiders both at work and at school. I was expected to be perfect with regard to these interactions as well. Email was only just starting to be a major form of communication at this time, and the web existed, but not in the form it is in today. Since I would of necessity give out my home phone number to any study group members, it was very easy for the leader of the home to monitor who was calling me. Why did that young woman call about the study group? Are you keeping yourself pure before God? Why did the coworker from the candle store call? Is something going on there? Spanish Inquisition-level interviews were not uncommon, but I was being faithful so I had a clean conscience.

Fortunately, there were regular small breaks where we could enjoy ourselves.

Remember the Arcata Assembly camping trip every August? Grizzly Creek Campground is on California Highway 36 east of the town of Fortuna. It is far enough from the coast that one can get decent summer weather. It's not guaranteed, however. The group would rent out a large camping space, and everyone would pitch in with food and other supplies. There would be preaching, swimming, and all-around fun. Huge redwoods, some with trunks in excess of ten feet in diameter, rise right up out of the campground and cover the steep hills nearby. This was a welcome change to the daily grind and gave me some hope that there would be opportunities to enjoy ourselves. Swimming in the river, hiking in the forests, enjoying some sunshine, all with some Bible study and prayer worked in ... this was a welcome and refreshing break from the grind that was breaking me down.

Next came the start of the fall semester which marked the second year of college for me. Going back to classes got the routine going, and between the recent camping trip and the busy schedule that school brought, my depression eased up substantially. In addition, fall brought the best weather of the year with clear skies and 70s most days. I began enjoying things a bit more, but the daily grind was real.

What is this daily grind I speak of? Let's go into the daily schedule I already mentioned in more detail.

Up early, 5:30 – 6 a.m., for morning devotional. All of us were encouraged to have a "morning time" with the Lord. Prayer, read the Bible, more prayer, perhaps pray with someone else in the home. Then breakfast with everyone in the home, and one of the single people living with the family would be responsible for preparing almost all meals. Meals together were a big priority. According to the founder of the cult, it was this failure of families to maintain traditional mealtimes and such that was a part of the breakdown of the fabric of American society. Often at these house meals, if there was no formal devotional, conversations would be led towards Bible topics by the head of the home anyway so there may as well have been a devotional. Then it was off to one's day. School, work, whatever. If school, one was encouraged to participate in the gospel table that would be set up on the campus. At the height of my commitment to the group, I was at the table nine hours per week. I was there so much that in my final year of college I was voted one of the three most recognizable faces on the campus by readers of the college newspaper. We were also encouraged to preach the gospel to random people we encountered during our day, so we always had a Bible on us as well as some Christian literature to pass out. After school/work/whatever, one would return home for dinner. Once again, most nights of the week it was expected that everyone in the home would be at dinner. There would almost always be a devotional.

In Arcata, Tuesdays and Thursdays would be meeting nights, with an additional meeting night on Friday if one was a college student. Dinner would conclude and there would be a rush to the meeting. Non-meeting nights could be spent however we wanted, but if you spent time alone you would be questioned as to what you were doing. One would also have daily stewardships around the house. These were essentially chores, but they tried to give it a spiritual element by saying that God had assigned this task in the house and as a result God would hold you responsible for doing it to the best of your ability.

Yes, as previously mentioned, they were literally teaching that God would hold you responsible for how well you cleaned a toilet.

Before bed, one was expected to end one's day with an evening time where one would pray, read the Bible, and consider God just like in the morning. In that way, one would begin the day with God and end the day with God. The reader can imagine, therefore, how it is that I came to read the Bible in its entirety eight times. Reading and praying both morning and evening during all of the years I spent in the cult resulted in many pages being turned.

Weekends were spent in similar fashion.

Saturday morning, we were expected to attend tape ministry at 7:30 a.m. This was a meeting where we would listen to prerecorded preaching from the group's founder, Brother George. It was a 90-120 minute affair, and there would be discussion afterwards. After tape ministry, we would have weekly chores to take care of around the house (as I said, God was apparently interested in how well we mowed the lawn and cleaned kitchens, too), and then there would be a weekly house meeting on most weeks where we would discuss how home life was going, anything we were struggling with, and of course have prayer and devotional time. Weekends were not for relaxation or recreation. They were more opportunities for work to be done. As mentioned, all brothers (in particular those living in communal training homes) were expected to prepare a possible sermon for Sunday morning. That is how one would end one's Saturday. Preparing a sermon that you may or may not give the next day, and praying with the other single brothers living in the home. If a single sister, you were encouraged to pray, read the Bible, and specifically pray for each brother in the Assembly such that God would lead in the preaching the next day.

Again, women were strictly forbidden from any and all preaching or leadership of any kind. Sit, pray, and cover your head with a garment to show your submission.

Sunday began with a morning time (and much trepidation about the possibility of preaching), breakfast, and then it was off to worship for the entire day. Worship consisted of people randomly praying out loud while we all stood, or requesting that we all open to a specific song in the hymnal we had. This random nature of worship prayers being lifted up or songs being requested resulted in many problems. Often, two or more people would start praying at the same time, resulting in people verbally running over each other multiple times each Sunday morning. It lasted about an hour. Then, we had the Lord's Supper (Communion), which lasted about thirty minutes.

Finally, there was about an hour of preaching time.

How did preaching work if every single brother was expected to be ready to preach?

Well, everyone would sit there and pray as ministry time was starting. Generally, there were three preaching slots to fill, one after the other. If you felt led to preach, you would just stand up and do it. There was no assigned preaching order, or topic, or anything. If you felt led to do it ... you would just stand up. Typically, the understood pattern was that the less experienced brothers would have the opportunity to go first and give a ten-or-so minute sermon. Since an inexperienced preacher would go first, it would give opportunity for the more experienced brothers who followed to correct any misstatements. The second preaching slot was taken by a more experienced brother, but not normally one of the leaders. This person was expected to add more depth in his sermon and to preach for about twenty minutes. Finally, the third preacher would stand and give an in-depth thirty-or-so minute sermon. It was almost always a leading brother, but on rare occasions one of the other senior brothers would be allowed to stand and preach that sermon. There were actually four preaching opportunities on Sundays, if one includes the five-or-so minute encouragement that was given just before the Lord's Supper. However, this was almost always a leading brother.

Strangely, even though Assembly members would tout the strength of this format for Sunday morning preaching and worship prayer, this setup is a bit of a case study in what was wrong with the Assembly as a whole. During every single open prayer or worship time, people would run each other over. Two (or more) people would begin praying at the same time, only one would finish that prayer. If God was truly leading each one, how could multiple people at the same time feel so led to pray or worship and cause confusion? If God was leading, then did he lead us to run each other over???

We were encouraged to be ready to preach. By encouraged, I mean if you were a man and you were *not* ready, you would get a talking-to. If you lived in a training home this talking-to could even include a warning that you would be kicked out ... uh, I mean, politely asked to move out if you were repeatedly not ready. However, if we were being led by the Lord, then why so often did multiple brothers stand up to preach simultaneously, resulting in one going up front and the others sitting down a bit embarrassed? If this was all the leading of the Holy Spirit, then how was it that so many of us felt led simultaneously? If God is omniscient and omnipotent, then there could only be one brother being truly led of the Spirit to stand and preach at any given time. Even the leading brothers (who were supposedly the closest to God and most in touch with His will) would do this, with situations often resulting where two leaders would begin to stand at the same time and one would be required to sit. Was the Holy Spirit confused? What was going on there? More of my thoughts on that later.

Basically, daily Assembly life was extremely busy. From sunup to sundown, one was expected to stay busy. Ever heard the phrase, "Idle hands are the devil's workshop"? The Assembly acted as if this was actually a biblical proverb.

It's not, in case you are wondering. It appears nowhere in the Bible.

However, the global leader was a firm believer that if you weren't busy then you were giving opportunity for Satan to temp you into sin. So, you needed to be busy constantly. You needed to be permanently fatigued. This way, you would be too occupied by God's work to be tempted and too fatigued to sin if you were tempted. He himself bragged about only getting four to five hours of sleep per night and spending nineteen to twenty hours per day in the work of the Lord. As a result, all of us were perpetually busy. My grades in college suffered as a result, too. Going to church five out of seven days of the week, with all the expected sermon preparation, devotional times, evangelism table on campus, training home stewardships, etc. didn't leave much time for studying for one's classes. Add to this the fact that extended vacations were generally discouraged, everyone was always busy in the "work of the Lord" and perpetually exhausted as well.

One other detail is that while we were laboring and pursuing and praying and studying the Bible and going to meetings ... other Christians we encountered expressed everything from mild concern about the group to outright accusations of cult status. At one point during my tenure in the Arcata group, a new person was getting involved. One of the campus police officers happened to be a Christian attending another church. He got wind of this person's involvement, got the contact information for this individual's parents, and called them to warn them about their child's involvement in the Assembly. Consider that for a moment. A university police officer, functioning in his official capacity, called the parents of a potential Assembly member and warned them that their child was joining a cult. The Heaven's Gate cult tragedy was taking place at this time, so the parents reacted with absolute panic.

We were working so hard. We were spending so much time in what we thought was service to God. While we were doing all that, we felt persecuted by the world around us, up to and including other Christians. Another example of this is the Lutheran Church in Arcata, which had a gorgeous location up in the woods. Given the view of the trees from this church's altar, it was a very popular wedding location. The pastor of the church at that time refused to allow any Assembly weddings at the site because he felt so strongly it was a cult.

I can also remember direct examples of professors, whether in science classes or some social class, who would both indirectly and directly address things they knew about what I was doing. "We *know* that evolution happens, and there is no doubt about that," all while looking me directly in the eye in a hundred-person auditorium. "We *know* that people are born with their sexuality, whether homosexual, bisexual, or straight"; again, all while looking me straight in the eye in a large classroom. The other students either chuckled if it was a science-based comment, or scorned me if it was a social comment. Interface with the real world could be really rough, but we managed it as best we could and were always able to return to our safe refuges. After all, we had THE Truth, so who were these lost sinners to mock us?

Daily Assembly life was tough, but we were taught that we were going the way of the cross and suffering as Jesus suffered. As we suffered, felt sadness, struggled with fatigue, sensed we were being persecuted, and generally believed life could be better, in the back of our minds the indoctrination kicked in and we believed we were being like Christ and would reap a rich reward in the end. All of us reasoned that this hard life was all going to pay off. There would be a rich reward in Heaven because we had seen something greater and were serving in vigor towards the fulfillment of the Vision. No matter how hard it was, it would pay off in the end.

At this point, I have to say a word about what I now understand to be the arrogance of it all. Consider this passage from Psalms 8:3-4 (King James Version) in the Bible: "When I consider thy heavens, the work of thy fingers, the moon and the stars, which thou hast ordained; What is man, that thou art mindful of him? and the son of man, that thou visitest him?" Look at the night sky for a moment. If you are in a major city, you won't get the full impact. In my hometown, at high altitude with dry high desert air, the stars looked like billions of grains of glowing sand scattered across the entirety of the sky. During a night with no moon, the sky was literally glowing with infinite points of light sparking in the darkness. I used to walk or drive out into the backcountry behind my folks' place where there are no artificial lights whatsoever and just stare upwards. Of all of the vastness of the cosmos, evangelical fundamentalists believe that the creator of all that vastness is focused on them at all times. Everything we see in the night sky is billions of light-years across, and people believe that in all of those innumerable spaces that the creator of all is singularly focused on them?

The arrogance.

Of all the innumerable stars in the heavens ... He is looking at me? What a self-centered view of the universe. Carl Sagan's view of this was *far* more humble. If you haven't read it, look up his words on the Pale Blue Dot photograph taken from the Voyager program. *That* is humility. Rather than the evangelical perspective that all of the vastness of the cosmos was created for and is focused upon us, we recognize our infinitesimally tiny part in all of this. Earth is all we have. We only have one opportunity. Don't fritter it away waiting for some divine wish fairy to "make all things right" in the end. You and I must do our parts today while we can, because this life is the only one we know for certain that we get.

As a testimony to just how busy we were, and just how deeply we were controlled by the group, consider what I've said about my love of the outdoors. Arcata is at the doorstep of an area called the Trinity Alps Wilderness. These mountains, though not as tall nor as massive nor as broad as the Sierra Nevada where I grew up, are actually far more wild. They are far more sparsely populated and there is much more wilderness there. There are areas up there where people just don't go. I never took a single backpacking trip, or even a day hike, into those mountains in the nine years I lived in Humboldt County. All of that wilderness at my fingertips, and I was busy going to meetings and hearing how sinful I was and how without the mercy of God I was doomed for an eternal torture chamber. "Oh the deep, deep love of Jesus," goes the song. Yes, a love so deep that if you do not believe in him, you will be tortured forever in a lake of fire.

As an adult, I have vowed that I will take the time to explore those mountains with my wife and son. It has already started. We took a camping/fishing trip to a small lake above the Klamath River not long ago. We will continue to explore these mountains as a family and will make up for the lost time.

Back to daily Assembly life ... a single forgotten chore was an indication that I was allowing some sin in my life. I spent so much time on my knees crying out for God's mercy. "Amazing grace, how sweet the sound, that saved a wretch like me," goes the song. The emphasis I saw more often than not was "wretch," not "grace." The Assembly left me continually feeling this sense of inadequacy, depravity, and dirtiness. Continually, I was praying for the mercy and love of God to fill me, and I was sad about where I lived and how little I enjoyed my life. Yet, at the same time I told everyone I knew that I had the joy of the Lord. In hindsight, I think a lot of people in my school and work life could see my unhappiness through the veneer I wore. This cognitive dissonance was true for a great many people in the Assembly. Crying out in tear-filled prayers for mercy and grace because we felt so guilty about basically everything, and yet somehow simultaneously walking around claiming "the joy of the Lord is my strength."

Another example of the spiritual implications of doing simple household chores is from the positive perspective. If you failed in a chore, then it is a sign of your overall unfaithfulness to God. If you succeeded in faithfulness to a chore then this was a sign that you would be faithful to God. Remember Luke 16:10 which I cited earlier in this chapter? Faithful in little then faithful in much.

I remember one day I was doing yard work at the home where I lived. The property was huge, and with the region's plentiful rain combined with mild temperatures, that grass *grew*. I had finished mowing the lawn on a day that had turned into one of those perfect Humboldt County days where it was sunny with temps in the mid-70's. While sweeping the cut grass from the crescent-shaped driveway, I paused to just breathe for a moment and look towards the ocean (which was visible from the house). As I stood there taking a few deep breaths of that salt-laden ocean air, a thought popped into my mind. Sweeping the driveway was doing God a service. I wasn't just doing a chore, I was serving the Lord. Since it was service to the Lord there would be some heavenly reward for the simple act of doing basic yard chores. Wow, imagine that! Eternal reward in Heaven for the simple act of sweeping!

Today, I realize how deeply indoctrinated I was to even begin thinking this way. At the time, however, we considered thoughts like this to be ennobling. In the Assembly, it meant to give nobility to a task, person, or other such thing that had no inherent nobility. Cleaning the toilet is a very ignoble task. However, in the Assembly there was an "ennobling" of such a task. Because cleaning that toilet was seen as an act of service for the Almighty God, suddenly there was great nobility in a task that was otherwise considered not only lowly but downright dirty. Mowing the lawn, cooking a meal, vacuuming the house ... all of these things suddenly became noble tasks of service that pleased your heavenly Father. Matthew 25:40 (King James Version) says, "And the King shall answer and say unto them, 'Verily I say unto you, Inasmuch as ye have done it unto one of the least of these my brethren, ye have done it unto me.'" Serving even one who is considered least in this world is equivalent to serving Him.

This thinking served two purposes in the Assembly. 1) It made us value simple chores to a much higher degree than most other people would because of that sense of noble service to God. 2) It made us more likely to accept the indoctrination of being perpetually busy since we would see this frenetic activity as heavenly service. The combination of these two factors made us all much more likely to accept control over our lives from the leadership, and more willing to sacrifice our time, energy, and money for the group. The perpetual business of our crazy schedules kept our lives constantly under the direct supervision of group leadership and simultaneously kept us in a state of mind that made us more likely to become even more deeply committed because we were thinking that everything we did was a service to God.

Speaking of money, what *about* finances? Basic expectations were that a minimum of 10 percent of your pre-tax gross income should go to the work of the Lord. *Minimum* of 10 percent. Remember, in the Assembly the minimum was *not* OK ... people expected everyone to go the extra mile in everything. Minimum effort was never acceptable. If leadership knew, for example, that you had just closed a very large sale at work and had been paid a very large commission or bonus, you would be approached about the potential of "giving it all to the Lord." The reasoning went that the Lord had given this money to you, so you could give it back to Him. Also, it was not uncommon for someone to sell an old car or other piece of property and donate the entire proceeds to the work of the Lord. Things like this happened, and to deny that fact is just dishonesty.

Basically, if any member received any kind of financial windfall there was a strong expectation that a significant donation to the Assembly would follow. Were there any audits or other checks of your personal finances to make sure you were giving at expected levels? No, there weren't. At least not in Arcata. In some Assemblies, I know that a part of living in a training home with a leader involved the review of your bank statements and finances to "teach you to be faithful with what you had," but that was *not* the majority practice nationwide. As a result, such donation enforcement did happen in some places, but it was the exception, not the rule.

Tithing in the Assembly worked like this. Cash-only donations. Zero checks. Zero anything else ... cash. Plates were not passed around for offering time. There, in fact, wasn't really an offering time per se on Sundays. There was a wooden box in the back of the room. The box had a little slit in the top. Cash was to be deposited in that box on Sundays, and *only* on Sundays. While (as I said) nobody audited your bank statements to see if you were giving or to verify how much money one made, if nobody saw you "going to the box" on Sunday, it would eventually be noticed. Also, if you lived in a training home, the leader in the home would watch how you spent your money. As I mentioned, this didn't necessarily involve some detailed review of your bank statements, but your behavior would be observed. In Assembly logic, clearly if one had lots of money for frivolities or entertainment or if one was eating out regularly, then one could be giving more to the work of the Lord. Did you go to a movie? First, was it a sinful movie? Second, that money could have been given to the work! Imagine all the good that the work of the Lord could accomplish with that money, but instead you decided to entertain yourself. Shame on you! These types of questions asked of your weekly (and even daily) routines were to be expected. On more than one occasion, one leading brother in particular directly called me out from the pulpit asking where I spent my money. Talk about shame-enforced behavior!

Weekly, two or three brothers (no women allowed) would go into the back of the meeting hall, unlock the box, take out all the cash, count it up, each would sign a document, and it would be sent to Fullerton for the work of the Lord. So far as I am aware, no copies of the documents sent *nor* other records of amounts sent were kept anywhere. Basic amounts would be withheld from the box to pay for local needs, like rent and utilities on the meeting hall. By and large, men in leadership were volunteers and received no compensation for what they did. There were a few exceptions to this in Fullerton and elsewhere, but the overwhelming supermajority of men in leadership received no pay. Aside from the small amount reserved for local financial needs, every last cent would be packaged up and sent to the Fullerton Assembly. What happened there, nobody in a locality really knew other than it was to be used for the work of the Lord. The only thing we know is that a similar counting practice took place in Fullerton where two or three would confirm what was received.

Having said that, no permanent records exist with regard to these counts, and the Assembly was *not* a formally registered religious group with the government, so zero accountability of any kind existed.

As for the Arcata group, I have complete trust that the people performing the counts did what was expected with the money. That, however, is part of the problem. I would wager that virtually *all* of the members of every locality around the world had the same trust and therefore did not feel any need to audit or verify the cash count. Here, once again, "just trust the Lord" came into play. As an accountant, I have significant experience evaluating internal financial controls, including public company financial controls required under the Sarbanes-Oxley Act. Two or three people were present when the box was opened. All of them confirmed the count. All of them signed a document. As far as that goes, this is a reasonable control (not perfect, but reasonable), and if one of them wanted to steal from the box, the other(s) would have been reasonably expected to report it. Having said that, here is my problem with that structure. There was no way for anyone in the local gathering to evaluate whether or not that count was accurate, or whether or not all of the cash made it into the package sent to Fullerton. We should have had a regular accounting of the cash. How much was collected? How much went to local needs? How much was sent to Fullerton? This should have been a part of a regular budget evaluation and report to the group as a whole, but it was not.

Anyone who tells you that you don't have a right to know how your money is being used has no right to ask you for money.

Period.

Other churches, nonprofit groups, and clubs like Elks Lodges have such accounting reports. Why not the Assembly? If anyone takes your money and refuses to tell you what it was used for, that is a *major* red flag. Just in case you think this is an uncommon practice, I can confirm that among many of the more fundamentalist evangelical groups in our country (in particular any group that says they are nondenominational), this type of lack in basic accounting is quite common.

The more significant problem, however, was what happened in Fullerton. Cash (yes, I must emphasize this again ... *cash* ... paper currency) came in from all over the country. I would say, "... came in from all over the world," but I actually don't know how international contributions were handled, so I can't speak to that. The brothers who collected the money would be quite clear if asked ... no accounting would ever be given of where the money went, or how it was used. At the 2002 Workers Conference in Colorado that I attended, one of the speakers said exactly that in exactly those terms. What do we know about where it went? There were a number of brothers who were full-time in the work of the Lord. As I mentioned, most leaders were not paid. However, those full-time in the work were paid. The international founder, George Geftakys, was one. Both of his sons (big shock) were two others. There were a few other brothers who were full-time in the work and whose families were provided for by regular deliveries of cash from these nationwide collections. IRS agents reading this are probably screaming at their books. Wait, what? Cash??? Cash was just sent to people? Untraceable? No ledgers showing how much on what date or what manner of delivery? It was just sent?????????

Yes, cash was just sent and there was no accounting of it whatsoever ... *anywhere.*

This practice was justified biblically, because of course in the Bible neither the priests of the Old Testament nor the leadership of the New Testament ever rendered any accounting to donors. However, basing a modern-day monetary practice on something that existed two thousand (or more) years ago is horribly misguided. "Just trust us" ... ahem, I mean ... "just trust the Lord" is not a good enough explanation of what happened to the money. As I said, there were some controls. Two or three brothers counted up and confirmed the amount of money in the box *before* it was sent so that the biblical practice of establishing things in the eyes of two or three witnesses (2 Corinthians 13:1) was kept intact. There was a similar practice where the money was received. However, modern churches should absolutely render an accounting to their congregations with regard to where the money goes.

The real deeper problem, however, lies in the fact that nobody (and I do mean *nobody*) knows exactly how much money George Geftakys, or the other leaders paid by the Assembly, were actually paid tax-free in cash over the roughly thirty years of the Assembly. Yes, you read that right ... all pay rendered to leadership was not only rendered in cash, but no taxes were withheld and the Assembly did not file any annual reports to the IRS nor any other organization because we were not registered with any government agency as an official entity, nonprofit or otherwise. No taxes were withheld from that pay *and* I happen to know (from conversations with some of those paid leaders) that they filed individual annual tax returns literally showing zero dollars in income. There is a section of each tax return for income from "religious service." This is where all of that money *should* have been reported on individual tax returns.

It wasn't. Zero was reported.

Also, registered religious groups are required to file tax returns as a legal entity that discloses what was paid to pastors, priests, etc. as part of maintaining their formal charitable organization status with the relevant governments. The Assembly never filed any such report because it was an unregistered group. A proper accounting of how much was paid to each person was not kept. Neither by researching tax records in some kind of discovery portion of a legal procedure, nor by researching Assembly records because there frankly aren't any, nor by researching individual financial records because so much individual finance was cash-based, will anyone ever be able to verify what was paid, when it was paid, or to whom it was paid.

Having said all that, we can come up with a conservative estimate of cash coming in by using simple common sense and some basic arithmetic. Here, I'll bring my accounting skills and experience to bear. Consider the following core assumptions:

- Approximately thirty years of cash donations coming in from a growing base of nationwide groups.
- Given, I accept that in the early years it would have been quite small since there was only one group in Fullerton at the beginning.
- Every member being told that 10 percent of pre-tax income was the *absolute minimum* acceptable percentage of one's income to donate *and* understanding that most people actually gave *more* than 10 percent because of the expectation to go above and beyond in all things.
- Local leadership in each individual group enforcing some kind of financial accountability with regard to those donations.
- According to the IRS, the median average annual US household income in 2002 (the final year of the Assembly) was $42,409.
- If the Assembly was a substrate of the basic US population, then everyone would have been plus

or minus that median, and we can apply it to households in the Assembly.
- 10 percent of that median income is $4,241 per household donated in cash to the Assembly each year.
- An average seminar in Fullerton saw 1,000 people in attendance (plus or minus).
- Since the average seminar saw 1,000 attendees, the total population of the movement in the US *must* have been an order of magnitude larger than that.
- Assume total US population of the Assembly measured in households, not individuals, is assumed to be 1,000 for purposes of this calculation (even though I would wager that is way too low an estimate).
- 2002 donations as measured by 10 percent of the median US household income multiplied by the number of estimated households is $4,241,000 in total cash contributions for one year (1,000 X $4,241 = $4,241,000).

I would argue that my estimate of over $4 million in contributions in 2002 is actually quite low. Even if we also assume that $241,000 (quite a bit of money) was kept by the local Assemblies to pay for local needs like rent and utilities, that still means $4 million sent to Fullerton in just one year.

All in cash.

All unreported.

All unverified.

All untaxed.

To repeat for emphasis's sake, that is just one year *and*

the calculation uses an obscenely low estimate of the total size of the Assembly movement nationwide. Also, that does not include anything coming in from Assembly locations overseas, if any, nor any one-time contributions like people donating the entire value of a sold car or the entire amount of a commission/bonus or other such windfall payment. At this point in time, eighteen years post-collapse of the Assembly, if anyone were to try to go back and account for that potentially vast sum of cash from over thirty years of operation, it would be an impossible task.

Do I believe that George Geftakys, or others in paid leadership positions, were unfaithful with the amounts they were paid? Yes. Yes, I absolutely believe that at least George and his son David used money in ways they should not have. When George took his "journeys" around the world to preach, he would stop for rest and recovery along the way. I have no doubt that some of these stops were more than a little luxurious. Also, his son, David Geftakys, in particular, had a garage full of expensive classic vehicle parts. Where did these parts come from? He didn't have income from outside the Assembly, which means at least some donations were funneled into his collection of classic parts and his extensive surfing habit, *not* into the work of the Lord. But, because of all of the reasons cited above, there is no way to go back and perform any kind of audit to verify anything.

As I sit here today writing this, I'm dumbfounded at myself. Why did I not question any of this? What caused me to just look the other way when there was a gigantic elephant standing right in front of me (and behind that elephant was an entire herd of other elephants)? How did

I throw myself lock, stock, and barrel into this with no question and no rational thought? I think I know the answers to these questions today, but it still boggles the mind that I was so incredibly committed to something so incredibly flawed.

To sum up this chapter, I can only say the following. We all went about saying we had "the joy of the Lord." However, underlying all of the smiles, all of the singing, and all of the "praise the Lord's," was this continual sense inside that we were full of vile sin, and that this suffering was our lot to earn an inheritance in Heaven. As a result, in many respects, daily Assembly life was about mitigating suffering. We all suffered the guilt. We all suffered the fatigue. We all suffered the frustrated desire of doing other more emotionally fulfilling things. We were all questioned and outright challenged by people from outside the Assembly, including other Christians. Yet, we stayed ... I stayed. Why? Simple. I wanted to please God and this was how I was convinced He would be most pleased with me.

Chapter Four
Progress and Promotion

I had a very hard time deciding what I wanted to do for a major. As I said earlier, I had originally intended to get a philosophy degree, go to seminary, and become a pastor. The Assembly did not believe in such things (remember, no paid professional leadership), so I needed to change my plans. I considered a number of other options including French, geology, English, and business administration. French because I could become a missionary to some French-speaking part of the world (I was thinking Africa). Geology because I was fascinated by it (I very nearly declared for this and took a large number of classes). English because I enjoyed writing and a stronger command of the language would help me preach better. Business because it was so practical a degree that I could use it almost anywhere to support myself. I declared as a French major briefly but jumped out when I realized I could, when it came right down to it, only do one thing for work as a graduate with a French degree ... teach. I did not want to become a French teacher. Geology would result in one of two viable career paths: 1) become a university professor and researcher, or 2) work for a mineral extraction company like an oil company or other mining company. Again, I didn't want to pursue the teaching route, so that was out, and I also didn't want to work for an oil company looking for new reserves to tap. Thus, despite how intrigued I was (and still am) by the field, I rejected the idea. English would result in a similar career path to French where I would be a teacher and/or possibly a writer. While I liked the idea of being a writer (heck, I am writing a book after all), I just didn't want to teach it.

At the end of the day, therefore, it was business administration that I declared for. This was during my third year at a four-year university. During the previous summer, my job at That Candle Store had to be abandoned as well. I had decided not to return home for the summer in 1997, and the retail store could not offer me a full-time job. As it turned out, however, this worked out far better since I got a job on campus as a maintenance assistant in the dorms. The pay was better and I was working on campus so I didn't have to drive forty-five minutes one way from the brothers home in McKinleyville to the mall in Eureka. Driving to school also meant driving to work. In the end it took me six years total to finish my bachelor's degree. That's way too long, but I was so busy, and transitioned majors twice, so it was what it was.

In the Assembly, I was doing well. My understanding of the core theological principles of Assembly doctrine was deepening, and my preaching was getting better. When the student who was leading the campus ministry (the same one who greeted me at the book table on the quad that first week I was there) graduated and moved on, I was chosen to replace him as the leader on campus. I would now be in charge of scheduling and running the gospel book table times (remember, nine hours per week), the weekly campus Bible study, and all other campus events.

The other students in the ministry would report to me and I would report to the leading brother in charge of the campus Bible study. At the same time, they began subtly grooming me for possible leadership in the distant future as a leading brother somewhere. All in all, I thought things were coming together.

My struggles with depression, an overall sense of dissatisfaction with life in Arcata, and my sense of being a worthless wretch continued full tilt and was strangely exacerbated as I rose within the Assembly structure. Just how bad did my perspective on my own wretched sinfulness get? On occasion, the inland mountains to the east would be the site of massive thunderstorms. On a clear night, these storms were so far away that you could not hear the thunder ... but the way the lightning would light up the clouds ... wow!!! Thunderheads would suddenly be lit by a silent violence of lightning in the distance. At one point in my tenure, I was so convicted by my own sense of sinfulness that just seeing this lightning terrified me. I was certain that this was another sign, like the avalanche, that a wrathful God was watching me very closely. I was utterly convinced that at any moment and for any reason this God might just decide to snuff me out. Former Assembly leaders, and other Christians, might say that this fear was a result of my lack of understanding of the grace of God. However, how can you read a story like that of Uzzah in 2 Samuel 6 and not fear? If this story was true, then this man reached out in purity of intention to steady the Ark of the Covenant ... and God struck him dead on the spot for trying to be helpful. This display of beautiful clouds being lit from within was not something to stand in awe and wonder over, nor did I think to stand

and admire the beauty, but it was something to fear. God was telling me to keep my path straight, or else. In Exodus, Moses would head up the mountain and the people below would see the massive smoke and hear the rumbling, and they would tremble in awe and fear. Just like in the Old Testament of the Bible where God would provide immense signs, in my mind he was doing this for me.

Another thing that developed over this time was my involvement in an acapella quartet. This was one of the highlights of my time in the group. Of all the things I did in the cult, this was one of the single most enjoyable. I had been in the church choir as a teenager, and now I was still singing. I never allowed myself to blossom or take full advantage of my voice because I believed playing second fiddle was an exercise in humility. Also, the leader of the quartet (no exaggeration) had a professional opera quality voice. Basically, playing second fiddle was the best I could do anyway when measured against him. He and I would become good friends. I enjoyed the rehearsals. I enjoyed the public performances. It was an area of relief amidst the stress of the overall group control experience.

The years progressed. I worked my job (which I enjoyed, overall) as a maintenance assistant in the university dorms, went to classes, and preached preached preached. As I worked in various dorm suites, rooms, etc., people began recognizing me as that guy from the Christian book table on the quad and I had lots of religious discussions with students. Neither my boss nor the other maintenance mechanics ever mentioned anything to me about my church involvement. If memory serves, it was in my fourth year that I progressed to the second preaching slot on Sundays at worship. During all of this time, I was faithful to the "no dating" standard. This was difficult in college. All around me were relationships, and not just among non-Christian people ... but virtually every other Christian group on campus had a dating scene. Not the Assembly. Having said that, I was still all in due to the way I perceived this teaching was helping me to resist sexual temptation.

My job, in the campus dorms, would provide some challenges in this regard. First, in the male dorm rooms I would often enter a room to fix a door, desk, drawer, light, whatever, only to find pornography sitting there. I would cover it with something, but the image would "defile" me, nonetheless. In addition, working in female dorms was also a challenge, in part because many of the student residents didn't wear much in the way of clothing while I was in the suite, and on more than one occasion I would be doing some work in a female bathroom and despite having a sign out front that I was in there, a woman would enter in a towel, or undergarments, or nothing at all and just step into the shower. Honestly, I think some of these occurrences were deliberate. As I mentioned, I was becoming well-known as "that Christian preacher guy" from the quad. Some of the "accidental" leaving of pornography out where I would find it, and women partially or fully undressing in front of me, was done with the intent to mess with me. "Take that, Christian!" or some other thinking process. Smirks I would receive from many of them seemed to confirm this, but I suppose I'll never know for sure. This didn't happen all that frequently, but it was enough that it formed a pattern.

Time moved on, I continued growing, and people in other Assemblies also began to show me some additional respect as I progressed. As the end of my fifth year approached, I began considering what to do after graduation. In addition, I left my job in the dorms and got my first professional internship as an accounting intern. This was a major transition for me, and it delivered me from the temptations that I mentioned in the prior paragraph. It was very different being in a professional business environment for the first time, but I really enjoyed it. Also, one of the leaders in the Arcata group was an executive officer of the company, so I got some real protection from the temptations of the world while at this job.

Regarding what to do after graduation, there were basically two options:

1. Get a full-time job and pursue marriage in the Assembly.
2. Go to the Campus Work in Fullerton.

I prayed constantly about it and considered what to do. The good friend from the acapella group I mentioned earlier graduated one year prior to me. He opted for choice #1. A specific sister was on his mind (also in the acapella group), and he immediately began pursuing his career as a teacher so he could build up the financial wherewithal to convince the leadership that he was ready to be a husband and father. His career path also served to vividly illustrate why I had not chosen to be a teacher and to reinforce in my mind the idea that my decision to pursue a business degree was the best one available. While marriage was at the forefront of my thinking (although I did not have anyone in mind at that time), I was feeling led towards option #2. One of the caveats to option #2 was that if you went to the Campus Work, you were basically forbidden from marrying except in very special circumstances for the entirety of your stay in Fullerton. Those very special circumstances were only ever available for children of prominent leaders in the Assembly, or so it seemed to me.

Despite the fact that former Assembly leaders may argue vigorously to the contrary, nepotism was a thing. Children of non-leaders would often feel "led by the Spirit" to participate in one ministry opportunity or other as they progressed into their teenage years. Very often these teens would be instantly shut down by leadership. This pattern would continue until the leader's own children reached that age. Once their own children reached that age, suddenly there would be a new idea received from God above. REVELATION FROM THE REVELATOR!!! Their teenage kids could participate in the various ministries! All the previous teens who wanted to be involved, well, it just wasn't in God's almighty time for them. The leader's own children? Gawd had spoken and now they could be involved. There were a number of different examples of this and, as one parent put it after the group began collapsing, the lightbulb almost never blinked on until a leader's own children came of age.

Oh, what was the Campus Work?

The Assembly's leadership heavily targeted cities with universities to be the site for new outreach. When the leadership was evaluating a city to start a new group, whether or not there was a university in town was a prime consideration. One of the mantras we heard constantly was that we needed to meet people with the gospel while they were young. You see, the reasoning was that as people aged their hearts hardened. Since older people had harder hearts they were less likely to accept the gospel of Jesus Christ and/or join the Assembly. Therefore, create new Assembly groups in college towns, and heavily focus your preaching efforts on the university. However, in order to create a club or other organized group on a campus almost every university requires that the head of said club be a student *and* have a professor as a supporter. Given that so many viewed the group as a cult, finding a supportive professor was actually really difficult. This was the reason for the Campus Work. It existed to train younger Assembly members in how to run a ministry club on their local university campus.

One of the interesting things about this is that the very strategy of targeting young people was a subtle acknowledgment of a principle of human psychology, but the group taught that psychology was of the devil. Older, more experienced people in general have better bullshit detectors with regard to ideological movements or groups that they themselves are not personally a part of. When someone who has lived a few decades happens to be an outsider looking in on a given organization or church or whatever, that individual is quicker (in general) to see any flaws and ask pertinent questions about it. Older Christians, university professors, and others often quickly diagnosed the problems of behavioral control and psychological abuse/manipulation (as well as other problems) endemic in the Assembly. This is why the Assembly focused so much energy on reaching young people. Because they don't have the seasoning of life experience, they were more likely to join the group. My youthful, enthusiastic, and idealistic self was the perfect target for this group. Take all of that idealism and energy and direct it towards the work of the Lord, and I would pour hours every day into it.

The polar opposite is true for people already IN a given ideological group or church or whatever. Adults that have been a part of any given ideologically based group for a long period of time are less likely to see things clearly, identify problems, and work to solve them. Adults whose minds have already been primed to accept given ideological principles are less likely to be able to recognize inconsistencies and problems. There were gigantic problems in the Assembly spanning everything from abusive practices, extraordinary control over the lives of members by the leadership, and exceptions to traditional Christian doctrine. If anyone questioned these problems, the typical response would involve layers of semantics intended to show that the control over people somehow was not really control. You went to see a movie and got Spanish Inquisition-level interview questions upon return to the training home you lived in? That's not *control*, that's *accountability*.

Also opposite of the principle with adults is that of youth. Where young people *not* in a given ideological group are less likely to see problems, those raised *inside* a given group are not only more likely to see things for what they are, they are more likely to call out the bullshit. One of the primary things the teen ministry (which I was involved in) in the Assembly was *constantly* dealing with was the fact that the teens (in general) spoke their mind about the problems endemic to the group. We were constantly, therefore, trying to convince these teens that control was not control, for example.

One lesson I have taken home from my experience in the group is this: if your child is adamantly questioning something that you take for granted, then it is a very good idea for you to take a big step back and re-evaluate that thing.

As an example of this phenomenon, where rational adults committed to a given ideological thing are not likely to see the problems within or rethink that thing, consider what is currently going on in the Catholic Church. It is now quite clear that the clergy (and I mean all the way up to the pope) has had full knowledge of the many pederasts in their midst. Not only that, but it is also clear that Catholic leadership all the way up to the pope has actively worked to conceal this horrific behavior. Did they immediately take action to 1) remove these people from their positions, and 2) turn over any individuals guilty of committing crimes to local authorities? No. They worked to actively cover up any and all wrongdoing, shame the victims into silence (even paying them off), and then they just moved guilty parties to other locations where they simply started over and victimized more innocents. Now, consider that not only has clergy all the way up to the pope been guilty of hiding this, but for many Catholics, this is a matter to continue to defend church leadership about. Catholics are not marching in the streets condemning these acts. I'm sure that many of the faithful are deeply disturbed by all of these revelations, but why the relative inaction? This is a perfect example of the very real phenomenon I'm talking about. Adults in the Catholic Church are not rising up en masse and taking action the way they would if it was some other group. Also, given the fact that (at least in the US) government tends to just keep its nose out of religious practice, formal prosecution is greatly lacking in this very serious situation.

Pedophilia is inarguably one of the single most disgusting, disturbing, and evil crimes that can be committed. Even with the evidence as clear as it is now that this is deeply endemic to the Catholic Church, the faithful seem reluctant to even talk about it. They seem reluctant to hold the leadership generally, and even the specific guilty parties, accountable. They seem supportive of the idea that the guilty parties should be protected/forgiven rather than prosecuted to the fullest extent of local law. Most disturbing of all, they seem intent upon somehow coming up with a way to blame the victims and continue the culture of shame and silence. Adults—otherwise rational adults—are making exception for one of the foulest crimes imaginable for no other reason than because their personal identities are tied up in the ideology of the church.

This is why Christopher Hitchens said, "Religion poisons everything."

Consider what would happen if we discovered that management and employees of a powerful multinational company like General Electric were doing what Catholic clergy have been doing. General Electric would face immediate and extraordinary consequences from the public *and* law enforcement. Investigations, inquiries, subpoenas, arrests—the consequences would be truly dire, and nobody rational would stand up to defend any cover-ups or ask that everyone just calm down, forgive the offending managers, and embrace some spirit of mercy. Religious ideology, however, informs different behavior and the adults in the church seem willing to grant lenience here that would be unconscionable anywhere else (and is indeed unconscionable here, whether they will acknowledge that fact or not).

This discussion may involve an extreme example, but the principle worked in the Assembly. George was granted special privilege in the group. He was allowed to do and say things that no one else ever would be. His behavior was just whisked away, and anyone who dared question him about anything would be disciplined. Adults in the group, by and large, just let things go that would never fly in any other real-world situation. One example is as follows: George would, in a sermon, talk about how grand the revelation he had been given was. He would brag about his ministry and education. He would toot his own horn loudly and often. Anyone else in the group (and I do mean *anyone* else) would be strongly disciplined for talking like he did. He proposed that he believed Adam was created by God on the seventh day of creation, when the Bible clearly indicates that it was on the sixth day. People just glossed it over. Anyone else who would suggest such a thing, especially from the pulpit, would be asked to stop it immediately and some corrective action would be taken. I can remember brothers who said things, either from the pulpit or in private, that were frowned on being pulled aside and corrected. Sometimes that correction would come from several people simultaneously. George could spout basically whatever he wanted whenever he wanted and just get away with it.

Adults would just let all of this pass. Young teens being raised in the group? Now, they didn't have the proper filters yet.

I was so convinced that this was *the* place where the

light was brightest, I just worked and worked away for the group without questioning any of the things I noticed. Most everyone around me was doing the same thing. Young people, in the prime of their lives, were pouring all of their energy into aggressive holiness, utterly convinced that we were serving God like we could nowhere else. Had we the necessary seasoning that comes with life experience, perhaps things would have been very different. As it was, however, we were all in. Older adults in the group, by and large, had come in when they themselves were young and had allowed their indoctrination to quash any serious questions that might arise. Kids born in the group, on the other hand? They would question everything, some of them without any filter whatsoever, as teens tend to do.

When it came time for me to make the decision, marriage or Campus Worker, I chose Campus Worker. I would put off starting a family and building my own life and career in order to serve the Lord on college campuses and work towards becoming a leader somewhere. Personally, I had a "burden" for the state of Oregon and there was a work just beginning in the city of Salem. I thought this was where I was destined to go eventually, but it would be years of faithful labor to get there.

As I mentioned previously, I never really liked Arcata. It was perpetually gray and damp, if not downright drenched. When the weather was good, it was absolutely perfect. However, that perfect weather materialized so rarely that it really didn't matter much. Having said that, I was also *not* a fan of Southern California with its crowds and smog and perpetual dry heat. I would be leaving an area where the only two seasons were the rainy season and the foggy season, and moving to an area where the two seasons were the dry and hot season and the slightly less dry and warm season.

One extreme for the other.

The move was uneventful, although packing everything I needed into my two-door 1994 Honda Accord proved impossible. One of the brothers brought down the rest of my stuff for me in a truck after I moved. I would spend the year on the campuses of Cal State Fullerton and UCLA. I had once sworn (after my family moved to Bishop during the summer of 1991) I would never again live in Southern California with its massive crowds and smog. A full decade later, in the summer of 2001, that's exactly where I began living. Would my childhood asthma recur? I was concerned about this.

Now I believed God called me to live in a place I despised. Did I love Arcata? No ... but it was worlds better than SoCal. I tried, when I could, to get away to the San Gabriel Mountains not far to the north, or to the San Bernardino Mountains to the east; however, I was so busy at all times that it almost never happened. The leader of the home I worked in hired me as an assistant of sorts in the engineering firm he worked for. I really liked him and his wife, and we bonded. Despite everything Assembly, here is yet another example of a couple that was influential in my life. People who I truly miss. I worked three days a week and went to the aforementioned college campuses two days per week. In addition to that, there were the normal weekly meetings typical of any Assembly group that I described earlier, although they were on different nights in Fullerton. I got out and went running when I could, but it was this year that my body went through a major transition from generally fit to generally lacking fitness. There simply wasn't time (nor did we have the energy) to devote any real effort to staying physically fit. The year passed rather quickly. I got away to visit family a few times and made it back up to Arcata for a visit once, but with one's nose to the grindstone so much the time really flew by.

Also, during this year, the first real tremors of scandal began to truly rock the Assembly. It was rumored, and on very good authority, that the eldest son of the group's leader (David Geftakys, whom I previously mentioned) had been obscenely abusive to his wife and children over the years of their marriage. He had allegedly beaten his wife bloody on more than one occasion when he lost his temper. He was a *very* muscular man. Type 1 diabetes ravaged his body, and to combat it he maintained a strenuous exercise routine. His muscles were large and cut. The idea of him letting loose on his wife and children is profoundly disturbing, even more so than typical stories of abuse like this, due to his physical size and strength.

These rumors had circulated for some years to one degree or another, but it was during 2002 that the stories reached something of a fever pitch. As the internet continued to morph into a larger and more accessible source of information, and a source that basically anyone could start a web page on and start posting, people began disclosing on online forums what they knew about David. The Assembly could control TV and many other sources of information. However, the internet was becoming available almost anywhere. I bought my first personal digital assistant during 2002 (it was an iPaq, if the reader is interested). Modern smartphones may put that device to shame, but it was such a novelty to have all of that information at one's fingertips at that time. This new arena of information sharing was something that Assembly leadership just didn't know how to handle. The typical, "just be quiet about it and don't ask questions" wasn't working anymore and the rumors really began to take root. Also, a mass exodus of Assembly members was taking place in David's home city of San Luis Obispo. These people had either been directly abused to a high degree, or knew someone who was abused, and they began adding their voices to the online chorus.

When other prominent leaders committed some sin or other, they were made to publicly repent in front of the gathered Assembly members. One in particular, in mid-2002, was made to publicly repent at the annual Workers Conference for something he had done. George's son David??? Nope. No such requirement for public repentance. Quietly and subtly just shift leadership around, keep him on the payroll, and try to keep everything under wraps. Special privilege for the Geftakys family, as usual.

As I mentioned, the hardest hit Assembly was the one where David was an elder, San Luis Obispo. However, outside of the SLO Assembly, things were kept very quiet indeed. People began leaving SLO like rats jumping off of a burning barge, including George's own grandchildren there. His grandchildren, having experienced such severe abuse, quickly made an exit. Even with that mass exodus going on, however, the leadership tried to keep it quiet. No public repentance for David Geftakys. Brush it under the rug and keep quiet about it. If you ask a question about it, you are given a curt answer and told to mind your own business (as I was).

I recall on one drive to the UCLA campus to go do

ministry, I asked David's brother, Tim (also an elder), about the situation. He said he believed that his brother had hit his wife "a couple of times" but that most of the rumors were just flat wrong. He seemed incapable of accepting that his brother could be as bad as he was. I was told to stop asking questions about it, told not to discuss it, and encouraged to pray for him. When I asked why there was no public repentance such as was required from other leaders, he said it was because it was a private family matter and told me to stop inquiring any further.

Once again, the Geftakys family got special treatment not afforded to others.

David continued getting paid after he was subtly removed from leadership. "Wait, but it's not the same," some may say. They always said that he was no longer getting money. However, he was being supported financially by George who was paid by the ministry, so ministry money was still flowing into his pockets indirectly. Recalling my earlier discussion of just how much money could have been flowing into the Fullerton Assembly from other locations, it should not be a mystery how David could have been easily financially supported by George.

The problem was not that both of George's sons were paid full-time elders in the Assembly ... the problem was that David, it was almost universally acknowledged, simply was *not* a good leader. He very clearly had a temper, his preaching was not very good, and he just wasn't a shepherd who cared for the flock. He was an authoritarian, even more intense than his father, who was to be obeyed completely. Failure to obey would result in swift discipline delivered in a spirit of profound anger. On the other hand, Tim (George's other son who I was working with on the UCLA campus) absolutely did embrace the spirit of a shepherd. When Tim was coming to your local Assembly to preach and spend some time, everyone looked forward to it. He was charismatic, he did not get angry, and the way he taught generally was with a spirit of understanding and compassion rather than his older brother's and father's spirit of authoritarianism. Now, as I mentioned earlier when discussing my asking him about his brother's spousal and child abuse, the general Assembly authoritarian spirit did in fact radiate out from him at times. Also, my more generous interpretation of his behavior was viewed through the Assembly lens. Compared to other leaders in the Assemblies he was more magnanimous. Compared to pastors of liberal Christian churches? Not so much. He would, at times, give you the typical Assembly leadership "obey without question" instructions. However, it was to a far lesser degree than many others. The teens, for example, would regularly discuss how they would far prefer things if Tim was in charge of the Assembly rather than his father George.

That year, spent in the Campus Work, was very challenging. From May 2001 until August 2002, I was busier than I had ever been in my entire life up to that point. Truly, the only time in my life that was busier than this year in Fullerton was years later during the two and a half years that I was working full-time and going to night classes to acquire an MBA. During that period from 2008 to 2010, I was commuting forty-five minutes one way in San Francisco Bay Area traffic, working full-time as the accounting manager for a start-up medical device company, and then turning around and going to night classes. This was the only time in my life that was busier than this year of Campus Work. Also, let's recall that the horrible events of 9/11 and the aftermath took place this year as well and those posed additional challenges to overcome. When you add to that the tremors of scandal that were only beginning to rock the core foundation of the Assembly structure during the same time, it was a very hard year.

Speaking of 9/11/2001 ... I had already planned to take a trip to visit my folks for a weekend. The weekend was September 14-16, 2001. The truly horrible events that I don't need to describe to anyone unfolded. Air traffic shut down over the LA Basin, but military aircraft flew constant patrols for many months afterwards. Prayer meetings and vigils were held. People came to Bible studies. End times prophecies were discussed at length. Then I took my trip. My folks and I drove up to the Bishop Pass trailhead at 9,700 feet above South Lake. It's amazingly gorgeous, by the way. As we walked up the steep trail, some backpackers coming out of the high country passed us on their way down. They were chatting about normal daily life and living type of things. After they passed, I turned to my parents and said, "I bet they have no idea what has happened since they hiked out into the woods for a relaxing trip." My parents both looked at me a little shocked by the statement, and then agreed that I was probably right.

Out there ... out in the woods ... human concerns seem to fade away for me. My mind is always running. If I have insomnia, it is because my brain just won't shut the fuck up. Thinking and thinking and thinking and thinking.

Random thoughts are always running through my mind this way and that. It's hard for me to focus on anything.

Not in the backcountry. When I'm sitting by a remote mountain lake, towering granite cathedrals all around me, the sound of the wind passing through the pines, water running over stones, birds in the air, my mind finally shuts off and the constant barrage stops. I can just sit and be. I can just close my eyes and have no thoughts cascading through my mind. This trip, with its little hikes into these amazing mountains, really reset me for what was to come and galvanized my spirit.

As these rumors continued to develop and it was becoming clear that there was substance to them, the rest of the world didn't really notice. At least, not yet. As the reader will recall, while in Fullerton I was working for the same engineering firm that the elder I lived with was an executive officer for. I once again lucked out, therefore, in the "pressures and questions at work" department. Nobody would get too pushy when one of the execs at the firm was an elder in the same group I was a member of. There were some Christian groups, as I mentioned, that considered the Assemblies somewhere between problematic and cult, but the group was so small in the larger scheme of things that leadership was able to keep the scandals contained to the Assembly itself for the time being. As a result, my family and other outsiders had no idea what was developing and there were no outside pressures aside from the normal ones I've discussed already.

I took a few hiking trips into the local mountains like Mt. Baldy and other places. I worked my ass off. I gained weight, going from the 150 pounds I had been since high school to 175 pounds. And I was further ensnared by Assembly doctrine. Having said that, it was this year, with the unfolding scandals and inconsistencies I saw in the behavior of George himself, that I began quietly asking serious questions. Two of the brothers who lived in the home that I did indirectly helped in my questioning. They just did not accept the directions they were constantly given. They began asking serious questions as the year progressed, and those questions undermined my resolve. I never said as much, and publicly continued to toe the line, but they helped me to see through the layers of crap eventually.

The year of training ended with a trip to Salem, Oregon for a missionary team during the summer of 2002. It was several weeks long and involved trying to establish a new Assembly in the city. Leaving the gray and brown of the LA Basin for the verdant forests of the Pacific Northwest was a profound relief. In addition, towering to the northeast, were two of the amazing Cascades Volcanoes ... Mt. Jefferson and Mt. Hood. This city was picked because there were a few families there who were associated with Assembly members in Sacramento, California. They liked what they saw in the group so much that they wanted a group to start in Salem. This city was an exception to the general Assembly rule because there was no major university in town. There were a couple of families meeting in a home, but the goal was to bring in a new group of converts and establish a core group that would be the foundation of a new Assembly. Once again, it was very busy, and the summer was (in my opinion) a complete failure. Nobody new came in, and the families we were meant to encourage ended up feeling exactly the opposite when everyone left. We had preached on the streets all over the city all summer, and there was literally nothing to show for it.

Late that summer, at the end of the missionary venture, I returned to Arcata and moved into the home of another leading brother. As summer progressed into fall, the Assembly leadership also started losing control of the scandal narrative to the point that outside people began hearing about it, and there was real pressure from within to deal with things more substantively. My family still had no idea, but other evangelical churches began becoming aware and this upped the pressure on the group profoundly. On a personal level, I had been trying to get Arcata leadership to allow me to move out on my own and live in my own home, but they wanted me to be more supervised. Just think about that for a moment. I had clearly stated that I felt it was time for me (a twenty-five-year-old man) to be on my own, make my own decisions, and just be a fucking adult for Christ's sake. Nope. Leadership nixed that. I would move into the home of another leading brother for at least a year as I performed campus ministry work at Humboldt State University and College of the Redwoods. This left me feeling rather like a child who needed to be watched rather than a grown young man in the prime of his life. I was not happy about it, but as the faithful Assembly servant, I agreed to it.

As it would turn out, however, my time in that home would be fairly short-lived. Tremors continued to rock the movement from within, and my life was beginning to change rapidly. A season of endings was looming on the horizon like dark storm clouds rolling off of the Pacific Ocean. Once again, I had no idea what I was about to get into.

Chapter Five
A Season of Endings

As this chapter title suggests, life began changing in profound ways in the latter half of 2002, and those changes (at least in my life) would continue to roll out over the next eight or so years. Strangely enough, although I call this period of my life "A Season of Endings," something else was just beginning.

During the summer of 2000, before I had left for the campus ministry and I was considering those two options (marriage or Campus Work), I decided to go for a walk on the beach and pray about it. As I have said earlier, the beaches in extreme Northern California are simply stunning: clean, free of crowds, with redwoods and Douglas firs running down to cliff edges and waves crashing over rocks as they rolled in from the Pacific. Trinidad State Beach is one such gorgeous location. This day happened to be one of those perfect Humboldt days that rarely graces the county—clear skies with a mild breeze coming off of the ocean, nobody on the beach, and waves crashing upon the rocks scattered out in the ocean. I sat upon a large rock on the beach and began reading my Bible, praying about what to do with my life. I was reading through the Psalms, and opening up my Bible I read the following: "Thou hast given him his heart's desire, and hast not withholden the request of his lips. Selah." - Psalms 21:2 (King James Version. The Psalm goes on to talk about a crown of gold on the king's head and destroying his enemies. This verse I interpreted as telling me who my wife was going to be in the Assembly.

No, logic was not my strong suit at that point in my life.

A cherry-picked verse about receiving one's heart's desire, in the context of a king's desire to complete the dominion and destruction of his enemies ... this was about me getting married. Not only that, but the sister that I believed God was speaking to me about was someone I would never have chosen to marry had we met outside the Assembly. From any natural perspective, I would simply never have been romantically interested in her ... nor she in me. I was also convinced that although God had shown me who he wanted me to marry, he wanted me to wait until after I returned from the Campus Work in Fullerton.

Thus, this season of endings was strangely kicked off by the beginning of something. The leadership had been talking to me about this sister. "She's a great sister," and, "She'll make a great supportive wife for someone one day," and, "Someone like her is exactly what a godly man needs," were some of the comments. She would later tell me that she was hearing many of the same words spoken about me. However, it was also made clear to me that if she was indeed to be my wife, I would have to wait until after I finished my commitment in the Campus Work. She also felt called to the Campus Work in Fullerton. Since we graduated from Humboldt the same year (2001) that meant we would both be going to Fullerton during the same time period. As discussed, that year in Southern

California passed quite quickly. Before I knew it, we were both back in Arcata. The leadership and I began talking about a potential marriage, but timing could not be agreed upon. I was told to just focus on the campus ministry and trust the Lord for the potential marriage. I also started my first full-time job in my chosen career field of accounting. Starting my career was a big deal. Not only was I starting my own career beyond the internship level, but I went back to work at the same company in Arcata where I had been an intern only a year prior, so it was in a familiar environment with a leader of the Arcata Assembly in executive management. Once again, I lucked out in the religious pressures at work department and wouldn't face any real challenges there.

What was marriage like in the Assembly? Good question. In my opinion, there were essentially three types of marriages in the Assemblies.

1. Natural healthy marriages
2. Fishbowl marriages
3. Arranged marriages

Natural healthy marriages were those that involved two people who might have fallen in love after meeting even had they met outside the confines of the Assembly. Two people were truly in love with one another due to a romance that might have developed completely outside the confines of rigid Assembly doctrine and control. Perhaps they might have met in another church, in a college classroom, in some kind of social club, or other such place. The setting wouldn't have mattered. These natural healthy marriages involved couples that were truly a good fit for each other and likely could have married happily outside the Assembly.

Fishbowl marriages occurred when two people were brought together because they had a desire to marry and start a family, but they were limited to the selection of people available in the Assembly. You see, marriage to anyone not involved in the Assembly was frowned on greatly (and that is an understatement). There were examples of individuals who were held in high regard prior to meeting the person who would become their spouse outside the Assembly. However, once these people started getting involved in an "unequally yoked" situation (see 2 Corinthians 6:14), this high regard quickly turned to judgment. In the Assembly, to be unequally yoked not only applied to being involved with unbelievers, but also to being involved with Christians who did not share the same "light" that we did. Pursuing a relationship with someone outside the Assembly was to break an unwritten rule that would incur some consequence in the group. Fishbowl marriages were a thing simply because we were limited to available partners inside the group ... inside the fishbowl. The massive ocean of potential partners outside the group? Not an option. Two people who would otherwise not be likely to choose each other (or perhaps would never choose each other) outside the Assembly ended up getting married to one another because it was simply a matter of the choices laid before them. This is where I would put my Assembly marriage. We, the two of us, would never have chosen to marry had we not been in the Assembly.

Thus, two people who just were not a good fit for a life partnership ended up entering into one anyway. Many of these examples of marriage from the Assembly, including my own, have since ended in various ways. Basically, when the one thing that brought people together was suddenly removed, there was no glue left to create adherence to one another. More on this later.

Finally, there were straight-up arranged marriages. To define my usage of this phrase more clearly, what I mean by "arranged marriage" is not that a father raised a daughter for the sole purpose of handing her off to a specific man one day (which has historically been a real phenomenon and is amazingly still happening in some parts of the world today). Nor do I mean that two people were outright told to get married when neither of them wanted to. What absolutely *did* happen in the Assembly, however, was obscene amounts of pressure being applied to people to marry, and normally it was a man who wanted a given woman and the leadership pressured the hell out of the woman to marry that man. There are specific stories that have been told, almost entirely by women, about a man who pursued her and how the leadership applied as much pressure as possible to ensure she would say yes whether she truly wanted to or not. This happened, and no amount of denying it by those who would dishonestly hide the truth will change that. It was shameful that people were pressured into life commitments such as this, yet it did happen. It was not very common, but the shame of coercing one person to marry another is something that deeply blemishes the Assembly movement.

As mentioned earlier, worldwide access to the internet was continuing to swiftly evolve. Now, devices like my iPaq could access the web on a limited level from the palm of my hand. With the advent of this new technology, the leadership lost a huge degree of control over what we all saw and heard. Scientology deals with this by providing computers (for purchase of course, not for free) that come with massive amounts of security software baked in which filters out bad news about the church and other information deemed undesirable by the group's leadership. In a day when virtually all news sources were in print or on TV, and we were all forbidden (unspoken rule) from owning TVs, controlling what people saw and heard was a far simpler task. With the internet, while we were taught to avoid pornography and other "defiling" things, they simply had no idea what to do about the rest of the general information. What about all of the open information sharing? They could inspect a home for a television and pressure people to remove it, removing that source of open information. But almost everyone had a computer at that point, and with all of those computers being connected to a completely open source of free information, we all began seeing things that leadership would rather we didn't.

Articles about the Assembly abuses that had begun appearing online in the year or two earlier started multiplying in huge numbers. They were articles written by former members of the San Luis Obispo Assembly (and other locations). Articles about the abuses of David Geftakys and others. I had discovered some of these articles while still in Fullerton, and this had driven my questioning of Tim Geftakys that I mentioned in the prior chapter. However, during late 2002 these articles began to appear in greater number and the accusations became both more direct and more detailed. As late 2002 approached, the impact of these articles had reached a fever pitch and the leadership of the movement realized that they could not keep it under control. The usual "just don't ask about it and stay quiet" approach was no longer working. The freedom of access to information online was simply too much for them to manage, and the information people were seeing was profoundly disturbing. People were asking very serious, very direct questions and, as I mentioned, the typical "just pray, trust the Lord and stop talking about it" instructions just were not sticking any more.

Back to me, personally, during this buildup towards late 2002; the leadership and I agreed that it was time for me to propose to the woman who I believed God had directed me to marry (as discussed, leadership had to approve such decisions, or the marriage would likely never see the light of day). Propose I did in late 2002, and we began planning our wedding for early 2003. Assembly weddings were viewed as conversion opportunities where visiting family could be reached with the light of the gospel and brought into the group. We sent out invitations to everyone on planet Earth with the hope that God would save some of the visitors and bring them into the group. However, while we were planning the wedding, the Assembly began to come apart at the seams all around us.

At the winter seminar 2002, George Geftakys was formally disciplined for his cover-up of the abuses committed by his son David. He was called before a gathering of leadership that included leaders from all over the country and had his power removed. He was not kicked out, but he would no longer be the global leader of the movement. Some (and by some, I mean a very tiny minority) of the leaders remained entirely committed to George and directly fought this decision. As a result, the leadership was fractured, and real infighting began in the movement. Some people still invited George to come and preach at their locations. Most, however, no longer invited him. This infighting would eventually result in a serious schism within the ranks of the Assemblies.

We continued planning our wedding as early 2003 wore on, setting a date for April 5th of that year. People began to slowly leave the Assembly in Arcata, while a core group stayed together in an attempt to reform the ministry from within and continue meeting as a functioning church.

As the leadership continued to fracture around the issues of his sin and new directions, George accepted an invitation to preach in San Francisco in early 2003 and went there against the wishes of the Fullerton leadership (where he lived). While he was away, a neutron bomb was dropped in Fullerton that would prove to be the final catalyst that would destroy the global movement. George Geftakys, it turned out, was not the holy man of God he proclaimed himself to be for all those years. He had, it was discovered, pursued illicit affairs with multiple different women over the thirty years of the Assembly's history (and, as it would turn out, had a history of doing so in other churches he had been involved with before starting the Assembly). Not only with multiple women, but often with women upwards of fifty years younger than himself. So, George had been guilty not just of hiding the felony child and spousal abuse perpetrated by his son David, but he had also been a sexual predator pursuing and taking advantage of naïve and idealistic young women in the movement.

The leadership in Fullerton decided to do the unthinkable. They excommunicated the founder of the movement in which they were leaders, and then they all stepped down from leadership stating that they had failed in their collective duties as shepherds of the group. The tectonic tremors that sent waves of energy through the various Assemblies had an immediate and devastating impact. One could just see the cracks eating through the superstructure of the movement. What had begun as a slow ebb of people leaving, almost entirely focused around San Luis Obispo, quickly morphed into a flash flood of departures.

Recalling my discussion about the types of marriages in the Assembly, the fact that people could be pressured into what were essentially arranged marriages was one of the primary ways George Geftakys was able to seduce women into inappropriate sexual relationships with him. His wife had a number of health problems throughout the history of the Assembly (and as it turns out, clinical depression was likely the cause of more than a few of these events). There was concern, on numerous occasions, that she might die. George would approach a young sister like this, "Sister, I believe that the Lord has spoken to me. When Betty dies, he is going to raise you up to be my next wife." The sister, having been trained that this was God's chosen servant, would be shocked but strangely honored ... even though he was decades older than her. Hadn't God raised up young virgins to comfort and care for King David in the Old Testament? Perhaps he was doing that here, too. He would ask her to pray about it and would begin pressuring her. Since young women in particular were trained that they were to be submissive to Assembly men, and more specifically to be extra submissive to leadership, the young woman would think it was somehow "sinful" or "willful" or "proud" or "arrogant" to say no or push back. As George's advances became more and more deeply sexual, he would lure them in. Since basically everyone in the Assembly, including leadership handpicked by George, had been trained to be deeply submissive to him, even if something odd was noticed about the way George behaved towards a given woman, nothing would be done other than to pray about it and trust the Lord. The fact that this happened multiple different times, and that it was *never* disciplined until the very end is a clear and undeniable example of how closely George controlled people's thinking.

In Arcata, we had heard the rumors. Hey, the internet was doing its thing. At the weekly prayer meeting one week early in 2003, the leaders read the letter of excommunication for George. The leading brother who was the central pillar in the Arcata Assembly (whom I had lived with for five years) wept as it was read. All of us wept. My then-fiancée and I were still planning our soon-coming wedding, but somehow that night I knew. Deep in my heart, I knew this was it.

It was all over. The Assemblies were dead in the water.

The movement might linger on for a while on life support, but it could not possibly survive. I spent most of that prayer meeting in tears as a result. I'm not sure if others there knew what I did, or knew why I was so upset, but I knew it was all over and that it was simply a matter of how long the movement would linger on barely clinging to life before finally dying off. My whole life plan had been laid out before me. I was sure that leadership was in my future, and that I would be sent to start a new location (I was imagining Bend, Oregon). I was sure that for the rest of my life I would be "laboring for the Lord" in this ministry. As difficult as it was for me in the group, there was still a very large part of me that needed to grieve the death of this thing that had been the central pillar of my life for nearly a decade. My life had been 100 percent invested in this enterprise. Heart, soul, mind, body, and strength. Now, I was absolutely certain that the life laid out before me was over. I wasn't the only one grieving, either.

People were angry.
People were confused.
People felt betrayed.
People were grieved.

People felt as if they were ships at sea with no rudder when we had all been so sure of our calling and future just days before. We thought that life's plans were confidently laid out before us. The Assembly was life itself for all of us. We ate, slept, and breathed Assembly life. For the rest of my life, I had envisioned serving somewhere in the world in this ministry. Now, all of those visions for our confident future were evaporating before our eyes.

It was at this time that I opened up to my family, both immediate and extended, about what had been going on. Everything just flowed out. My retired police officer father was adamant that criminal charges needed to be brought, particularly against David, but none of the events were in his jurisdiction. I told them that I would continue on in the Arcata Assembly, but that we would reform it. We were still biblical literalists, which they did not agree with at all, but they were comforted to some degree that the truth had come out and people were moving forward. My folks, as it would turn out, had spoken with their pastor about this many times. This was the same man I had been so inspired by as a young man. He had told them that much like the dream in the book of Daniel, someone in the Assembly would be found to have feet of clay. The whole edifice would collapse. I would be fine. While my parents took the revelations as events that would send me in the right direction, others were not so passive about what had happened. The pressure from outside Christian groups increased markedly. This would get really challenging on the university campuses where we were trying to recruit.

There really were two major categories of reaction to everything that transpired. The predominant reaction was to accept the truth of the accusations against George and David and to begin questioning everything that was held dear. How could God have spoken through such a man? We thought we were hearing from God, but could we really have just been deceived since these facts about his real life came out? The other reaction by a select few, like those in San Francisco, was the polar opposite. These were so convinced that God had indeed spoken to them that they believed all of the accusations must be false. No matter how much evidence was amassed, it was believed that it all must be false due to the perception that God had spoken. Since God doesn't speak through evil men, went the reasoning, then George must not be evil. More on this later.

One of the things that upset me so much was that I thought I *knew*. KNEW how the world worked. Knew what the almighty God wanted. Knew where my life was headed. Knew how my life should be ordered and managed. I thought I knew, and I was 100 percent confident in that knowledge. Now, as I began to question, the unknowns began to eat at me with a maddening intensity.

As all of the news fully spread through the Assemblies, we had many more meetings about what had happened, where we were, and where we would go from there. Shepherd, who had discipled me all those years earlier, was livid during one of the meetings. Upon hearing that David had so horribly abused his wife and children, Shepherd said something along the lines of, "My money has been going to support this man! What is going to happen about this?" Around that same time, one of the brothers who had been in the ministry for decades decided that he and his family were leaving. They were the first out the door, but they were not the last.

The truth of these matters was quite difficult to accept. How could we all have ignored all of these warning signs for so long? Why had we all gone along with the control and abuse? Now that it was clear that the man who we had all believed was this holy revelator of divine truth was in fact nothing of the sort, we began to question many of the things we were taught. As I mentioned, my then-fiancée and I decided we would stay on to attempt to reform the Assembly from within. No longer would we be a controlling group. We would evolve.

As a testament to our desire to change, the leadership actually invited pastors from other churches to come to our meetings and counsel us about how to go forward. We heard a number of diverse perspectives. Numerous questions were asked. However, in hindsight I realize what was happening. We had all been trained to be led by authority figures. Here we were calling upon authority figures to tell us what to do. Same problem, even if it appeared different.

As the time of the wedding approached, leadership in the Arcata Assembly began to step down and leave the ministry. The first leader to leave was the one I had lived with for so many years. He was devastated by it all, as was his wife. Being the cornerstone leaders in Arcata, guilt over all the hurt caused and missed opportunities with their own children was just too much. They felt so deeply and personally responsible for all of the pain caused in the ministry *and* they had their own wounds to bear and heal as well. The only solution, they reasoned, was to dissolve the entire movement. It was too full of problems, so woven into the fabric of everything we did, to be saved. There was no way to evolve. They left and pursued healing elsewhere. Others soon followed family by family, and individual by individual.

Our wedding day arrived, and it was actually pretty uncomfortable. Many of the people from San Francisco were there ... the same people who refused to accept George's excommunication and still allowed him to come into their midst. These made a point of wandering around telling people how unfaithful they were being by leaving the movement. At one point, the leader of the San Francisco group approached one of George's female accusers and told her flat out that she had no evidence, she was a liar, and she needed to just be silent.

Not appropriate wedding behavior.

When we were married, we were living with one of the remaining Arcata leaders and his family. However, it became quickly apparent that this was not going to work so we moved into our own place. It was a little duplex on the edge of the forest. A short run up the road, and we would be on a trail in the forests of Humboldt County. I still choke when I realize we paid the tiny sum of $700/month for our 1,000 square feet of the duplex. The Assembly continued to disintegrate all around us, but we strove onward. One by one all of our closest friends vanished. We would still see them around, go to BBQs and other gatherings, and try to keep in touch, but it just was not the same.

The wiring that had once connected us together so tightly, had provided such a strong charge to everything we did, was simply gone. There was just too much baggage.

Our mutual experiences of abuse, control, and indoctrination were (in the end) just too much of a hurdle to overcome. As the end of 2003 approached, it became quite clear that the Arcata Assembly was doomed. So many had left and moved on. So much pain had been endured by all of us. There were just a few left by the end of that year.

Early in 2004, we left. When we did, the few that still remained after us decided to close up shop and move to other churches in the area. That was it. Nearly a decade of my life spent in this group (August 1995 to January 2004), and it had come to nothing. Today, there are still some from the Assembly that I keep in very light touch with. Having said that, none of my former friends (brothers and sisters in Christ) remain close today.

All of the people that I would once have given my very life for have drifted away.

At the same time, the larger belief structure that was my faith began to change. At first the changes were subtle, but as the snowball rolled downhill it gained more and more mass over the passing years. Just like one of those death cookies in the avalanche so many years before, even a tree that had stood for millennia would be mowed down instantly if it was hit. This first step was reasonably simple. I had believed that Almighty God had called me to personally support the leader of this group, George Geftakys, much like the Apostle Paul had his workers that accompanied and supported him as he traveled and preached in the book of Acts. Not only did I believe this, but there was confirmation of the Holy Spirit because many others believed the same thing—others confirmed that this was indeed my calling. However, my reading of the Bible was quite clear. God does not call people to support men who are sexual predators. In fact, 1 Corinthians 5 is an entire chapter of the Bible devoted to instruction on the excommunication of people who engage in what is called gross sexual immorality. My belief that Almighty God had called me to support a man who turned out to be a sexual predator could not be true. I must have been deluded. I simply *must* have been wrong. God simply would not have called me to support such a man. The others must have been deluded, too. A seed of doubt was planted in my mind. If I was deluded about this fervently held belief, a belief close to the core of my calling as a Christian, what else could I be deluded about?

Over the next few months (in the first half of 2004), we attended Arcata First Baptist Church, one of the most successful in the city. The time there was good for me, but I was still very much feeling like a ship without a rudder. What did God want for my life now? Where was my future headed? Now that I was married, and still believed that a man is to lead his wife, how was I going to guide us along this completely uncertain path? In addition to my sense of being without any direction, there were members of that church who simply could not accept me. I had abused them over the years and they remembered. This resulted in every single service being one in which I felt like not everyone present wanted me there. Fortunately, my career was developing, and within a few months of accepting my first full-time accounting job I was made a team leader. This was a huge step for me. However, I remained very unhappy in Humboldt County. Also, less than a year after our wedding day, our marriage began showing the first signs of decay that would lead to our eventual divorce years later. Finally, in addition to the lack of acceptance I felt at local churches, and the fractures already appearing in my marriage, people at work began gently asking questions about how things were going. Everywhere I went, it seemed, this shadow followed me.

As I mentioned, my then-wife and I were a fishbowl marriage. We never would have come together had it not been for the Assembly. Once that influence was gone, the fabric that was our relationship began coming apart thread by thread. Given all of these things: lack of a place in a church, loss of our life's guiding direction, and uncertainty about where to go, we needed to make a change. Therefore, in July 2004, we made the move to San Leandro, California, partly due to some needs in my then-wife's family. We moved into her grandparent's old home and became caretakers for it.

Despite hating the constant gray and wet of Humboldt County, moving to a Bay Area city just south of Oakland, where emergency sirens were almost as common as the banshee howl of the BART (Bay Area Rapid Transit) light rail cars, was not what I had in mind either. I was really unhappy there, too, but was determined to make the best of it. We moved in, and began painting and doing other things, mostly with the intent of removing the smell of decades of smoking from the house. It was a long process and combined with the overall dissatisfaction with the new area, life became very unhappy. However, my cult conditioning was still very much in place and I told myself that this was the cross of Christ and this was what he wanted. During this time we also began church hopping, not really feeling at home anywhere and searching for an environment that felt right for us. I wouldn't realize just how dreadfully unhappy I was in this house until years later.

After a couple of weeks, I began looking for a job. I got a temporary placement as an accountant for a cemetery (yes, I said accountant and cemetery in the same sentence ... just imagine the tedium). The people were very nice, but this was a dead-end career opportunity. I would learn nothing new. I would have no challenging business situations. Emotionally it would be very trying dealing with grieving families every day, but from a business standpoint this was a cakewalk for someone who never wanted to be either challenged nor highly compensated. I spent my hours doing menial accounting tasks (mostly cleaning up the mess left by the last person in the position). The cemetery itself was actually quite peaceful, which is what they are supposed to be. More than a little bit of my time here was spent in quiet contemplation of the recent events in my life. I would go for walks on break times and watch squirrels doing squirrelly things and listen to the Bay Area breeze in the trees ... but I knew this was just a pit stop along the career journey and more challenging opportunities awaited.

After only two weeks there, I found a permanent opportunity. It was for a home water purification company that sold filters designed to be hooked up to the main water supply of the house. They would hook up their super water filter (using technology that was quite literally used inside the space shuttle), and the entire home would be supplied super purified water. I was very excited to be working for what looked like a great company.

Then came my first day.

I came in and was immediately slammed with a huge workload including (yes, you guessed it) a major cleanup job from the person who had previously held the position. The accounting was a mess. There was a consultant there who had been hired to help bring things into order according to Section 404 of the Sarbanes-Oxley Act of 2002 (SOX 404; the reader can look up the Act online), since the parent company was publicly traded. On the first day I sat in my cubicle listening to quite literally everyone around me bitching about their jobs. One individual said, "You know, I used to like working here. It used to be great. Now I hate this fucking place." Yeah, that was my first day and those were the kind of statements I overheard all day long.

Everything went downhill from there. The CEO was a complete dick who took no personal responsibility for anything and shouted at everyone all the time. In my entire career, this is the single most horrible person I have ever worked for. I worked my ass off. I poured in massive hours. Cleaned up major portions of the accounting.

Worked to establish internal controls that actually had real practical use. Got yelled at, condescended to, cursed at, and watched some of my coworkers go through worse. More than one person nearly had a nervous breakdown working for this complete piece of shit. The parallels between spending years in an abusive cult situation with dictatorial leadership, and then transitioning to a dictatorial work environment, are not lost on me. The product this company manufactures is truly a great product, top tier in its segment. The culture, however, was abysmal.

It was a very rough two years from 2004 to 2006.

The company I started working for was acquired by a large multinational, and shortly thereafter the CEO took it private again. Yes, I started working for one company, it got acquired by another, and finally went private in a third. I literally worked for three different companies all while sitting in the same chair in just over two years' time. I started as the accounts payable accountant and was promoted to senior accountant about a year in. In the end, I simply could not stand it any longer and resigned my position in order to move on. I didn't have a new job lined up yet, but I was at my wit's end. I took the risk and jumped ship.

I related this experience because, in a sense, that sums up the Bay Area for you. Go to work for a company, it gets acquired, move on to the next company. Like a game of musical chairs all while dealing with strong personalities, both charismatic and anything but.

During my tenure at this hellish company, my marriage was continuing to slowly deteriorate. Despite that trend, we actually ended up purchasing the home we were living in during 2007. This was a decision that we would soon regret as the entire economy collapsed during 2008 and we lost more than 50 percent of our equity in that home. We began seeing a therapist through the church we were attending at the time. She was very nice and very helpful. She really helped us to take a big step back and look at our situation with new eyes. Why had we come together? Were we really attracted to each other? What did God want for us now? Since this was a Christian therapist provided through the church denomination, what God wanted was a priority question. It was during this time that both my ex-wife and I realized that we had been in a fishbowl marriage. Had it not been for the Assembly, we would never have chosen to marry one another. This revelation was incredibly important. I am a firm believer to this day that in order to chart a proper course for your life, you need to understand your past very clearly and you must be brutally honest with yourself about everything.

When considering charting a course for one's life, I like to use the analogy of a map. Given satellite-based navigation systems today, this is not much of an issue for people anymore. However, I'm old enough to remember trying to navigate a strange city with a paper map. There are, in my opinion, three pieces of information necessary when using a paper map. The most important is *not* where you want to go ... your destination is *not* the most important thing. The single most important thing to know is this ... where are you right now? It doesn't matter if you can find your end destination on the map if you can't identify your current location. How can you chart your course to that goal unless you know where you are right now? This is why I said that it was so important for my ex-wife and me to realize where we were in our relationship. How could we even begin to chart a course forward if we didn't know where we were?

Back to the analogy, the second most important piece of information is where you want to go, and the reasons for that should be obvious. If you want to reach your destination you obviously need to know where it is on the map. If one knows where one is on the map, and one knows where one wants to end up, then one can chart a course. Finally, there is a third piece of information you need. That third piece is where you started your journey. If you can understand where you made wrong turns, where you got confused, where you became misguided in your journey ... this knowledge will help to prevent you from becoming lost or misguided again in the future.

Where are you now? Where do you want to go? Where did you start?

My ex-wife and I spent a lot of time talking about this reality, and when the therapy sessions came to a close, we had a new view of where we had been and where we were. Finally, we were both willing to use the word "cult" with regard to what we had been involved with for so long. It was (to cite Dr. Richard Dawkins) a "consciousness raising" moment. After that realization, everything in the world suddenly looked very different to our eyes.

We would never have chosen to marry had we not been in the Assembly.

This thought was so important to realize because it allowed us to better see how we had become lost and misguided in our past. However, it left us with a question that (as people who were still pretty conservative

Christians) was quite difficult to answer. Even though we would not have chosen to marry one another, nor would we have fallen in love had we met outside the rigid confines of the Assembly ... the fact was that ... well ... we *were* married. Despite the realization that it never would have been without the cult control, we were a married couple at the moment, and we had a very serious decision to make. Would we stay married and try to work out our differences, or would we go our separate ways?

This confluence of events provided quite a challenge. As I was making a major change in my professional life, I was also facing a quantum shift in the substance of my married life. In the end, we decided to press on in our marriage and continue to work on things. However, the reality was that our relationship just continued its slow downward spiral of deterioration. My ex-wife and I both weren't truly happy at the church we were attending (she, as a matter of fact, just stopped attending at some point along the way). I kept going because I was holding onto the fabric of the "known" with true grit. I was desperate to keep this familiar environment in my life, so I held on ... and did so much longer than (in hindsight) I should have.

Professionally, I was so shell-shocked from the experience at the water purification company that I took four weeks off to recover. After the four weeks, I began looking for work again and found a *great* job that I truly loved. I went to work for a biotech start-up. The culture was amazing. The people were Top-notch. The technology under development was very exciting. All in all, this was one of the most amazingly positive career decisions I have ever made. I started at the company in August 2006 as the senior accountant (my title carried over from my last job). Here, I put into practice many of the things I learned at my former job. Even though I detested the former work environment, being dumped in and forced to invent things for myself taught me a tremendous amount. In addition, it was an environment where I was outright encouraged to take the time to educate myself and continue to broaden my knowledge base and skill set.

From a professional perspective, things couldn't have been better.

After working there for about a year, I applied for the MBA program at California State University, East Bay, and started that program in January 2008. I was working in a great environment full of intelligent and positive people, and I was starting the next step in my education that would further propel my career growth. By all appearances, everything in my life simply overflowed with success. Nobody knew, however, that during this same time period my marriage was steadily rotting away from the inside out. We had begun seeing another therapist ... this one secular. During these sessions we heard the following question for the first time:

"Do you think you guys should remain married, or is divorce actually the best option long-term for both of you?"

We both took this question very seriously. Conversations about what a divorce would look like became a very regular occurrence in our home as 2008 progressed into 2009. We didn't really do much during this time in our lives. We tried taking a few short trips together to see if we could re-spark something between us, but to no avail. I began to realize that divorce was inevitable and I started grieving that coming reality as a result.

Unfortunately for the biotech start-up, the Great Recession took place in early 2008. As a start-up, the company's continued existence as a going concern depended on regularly conducting fundraising efforts in the public stock market. The fundamentals of the business were sound. We had just concluded a successful phase 1 human clinical trial for our keystone product, and we were getting very good initial animal study results on some additional applications of our technology. However, when we went out into the market to raise money on the back of our successful human clinical trial data in spring of 2008, the market was in freefall and the worst recession since the Great Depression was well under way.

The financing attempt failed.

Nobody was willing to invest in a start-up like ours in a market environment like that. In the third quarter of 2008, the biotech start-up declared Chapter 7 bankruptcy. Unlike Chapter 11, where a company can reorganize debt-free and start over, this meant that there would be no reorganization attempt. The assets of the company would be liquidated, and we had no choice but to close shop.

I was really struggling with failures at this point. The company I worked for had failed. My marriage was failing. I was failing to find a church home where I truly felt that I belonged. The bankruptcy of this company was just another blow to my ego and fueled my downward spiral.

Fortunately, the controller and I had gotten along really well. He had already left shortly prior to this and was working for another start-up with a great product called "the medical device." This company was very well venture capital funded, and it was private so there were no public company concerns to deal with. I accepted a position with that company that started a mere week after my Chapter 7 bankruptcy layoff date at the biotech start-up.

I was progressing with great success through my MBA program. I essentially got a week off of work, and then started a new job. I also went from senior accountant to accounting manager and received my first six-figure base salary (not including bonus). This was another great cultural fit for me. I was working for a manager whom I respected very highly and with whom I had a history. Also, the two gentlemen reporting to me were great people who worked hard and knew how to do their jobs.

As 2008 progressed into 2009, my personal life continued to fall apart. I was commuting an average of ninety minutes per day round trip from my home in San Leandro to the medical device start-up in Santa Clara. That commute took a huge emotional and physical toll on me. My ex-wife moved out of our home and into a friend's home late in 2009 as we pursued a separation. I remember crying while standing in the middle of the street one night as she drove away.

- Where was God?
- I was praying desperately for the success of our marriage, but it continued its downward spiral. Why?
- I was serving without pay in the music ministry of a church, but why was I so skeptical about that church?
- What on earth was I supposed to do?

I was also attending night MBA classes and that stress was continuing to pile up on me, despite how well I was doing in the program. My average schedule on a day involving night classes was to be up by 5:30 a.m. so I could commute to work prior to traffic buildup, and so that I could walk my greyhound, Lucy, before I left. Work would run from about 7:30 a.m. to about 4:30 p.m. depending on how morning traffic treated me. I had to leave work by 4:30 p.m. on a class night to guarantee I could actually make it to class through the traffic and still find time to eat. On a non-class night I would stay at work later. I would have dinner somewhere in Hayward around 6:00 p.m., arriving at class at 7:00 p.m. Classes generally ran from 7:00 p.m. to between 9:30 and 11:00 p.m. depending on the professor involved and what their teaching style was like. I would arrive home between 10:00 p.m. and 11:30 p.m., crash out, and then be up at 5:30 a.m. the next morning. Adding in separation/divorce stress on top of that made life extraordinarily tiring and stressful, despite my professional and educational success. Add in stress-fueled insomnia to boot, and things were really tough.

As 2009 progressed into 2010 my ex-wife actually ended up moving back in for a few months because things did not work out between her and her former friend. This made the home situation extraordinarily awkward. I had done almost all of my grieving for the end of our marriage while she was living with her friend, so having her move back in was actually a bit of a step backward. It was also particularly awkward because she began seeing another person romantically during this time when she was still living with yours truly, her soon-to-be ex-husband. That prompted another step in the grieving process for me, and it would turn out to be the final step.

Bright glowing light alert!!! Then came a day I had worked towards for two and a half years.

On the 12th of June, 2010, I was awarded my degree of Master of Business Administration - Accounting Option. My long slog of night classes was over. I had graduated with a 3.7 GPA (an A average!) which was the highest I'd ever achieved in my life, and I had done so while working full-time in a management position for a Silicon Valley start-up, commuting upwards of ninety minutes per day, and going through a painful divorce. In my entire life, I had never worked so hard before, nor have I since. Even the IPO push in 2013 for my current job pales in comparison to the workload I shouldered during the two and a half years from January 2008 to June 2010. To celebrate, I attempted to hike to the top of the tallest mountain in the lower forty-eight United States ... Mt. Whitney. The previous winter had brought then-record snowfall (due to climate change, the record has been repeatedly broken since then). The snow, combined with poor acclimatization, caused me to fail in that attempt. I was hugely disappointed, but it was another great learning experience.

Also, I just love being in the mountains, successful summit bid or not.

However, the MBA wasn't the only chapter of my life to close. In August 2010, my ex-wife moved out of our home permanently and formal divorce paperwork was filed. My fishbowl marriage was also over and since I had already gone through the grieving process in the prior few years *and* my ex-wife was no longer living in the home, I considered moving on. I had many questions circulating in my mind.

I'm thirty-three years old; will I be able to find anyone amazing at this age or will I have to settle?

How do I even start dating? Because of the Assembly, I literally had not been on a single date (barring with my ex-wife) since high school. How the heck am I supposed to just go start dating again? Since I had never dated in my entire adult life, would I even know what that the hell I was doing on a date?

What will happen to this house I live in? I'm so far underwater due to the recession that I can't even see the surface anymore! Why did I agree to purchase this thing in the first place since my marriage was so far out on the rocks at the time? Am I stuck here in this house that I never enjoyed living in anyway?

What do I believe at this point? I still attend the church where I've been leading the singing for a few years, but what exactly do I believe? I didn't even know, really. I still believed in God, but what theological positions did I even hold anymore?

Am I consigned to be single and living in a house that I'm miserable in for the foreseeable future?

These questions and more circulated in my mind and I didn't, as of yet, have an answer. A season of endings had come to a close, and with my grieving done, I was now looking ahead to the potential of new beginnings. I just didn't have any idea how my future would unfold.

Chapter Six
A Season of Beginnings

Living alone took some getting used to. I had my greyhound to keep me company, and Lucy was truly an amazing companion. As an aside, if you are interested in rescuing an amazingly affectionate breed of large (lazy) dog, consider a greyhound. I kid you not, Lucy slept eighteen to twenty hours per day. She required one walk per day, and one or two episodes of "zoomies" in the backyard or fenced outdoor area, but otherwise she was just a sleepy and super affectionate dog. The breed has rightly been labeled 40mph couch potatoes. Now that I wasn't attending night classes, I walked her every evening when I got home from work (and since I was accustomed to getting up early, sometimes in the morning too). I played lots and lots of video games. My Xbox 360 got tons of mileage through this period (*KOTOR*, *Dragon Age*, *Mass Effect*, *Gears of War*, and *Halo*), as did my PS3 (*God of War* and *Uncharted*). Leading worship singing at the church I had been attending was also still a central part of my life, though I still struggled with a sense of not belonging.

The medical device start-up had been acquired in late 2009 by a large multinational company. Shortly after the medical device start-up acquisition was completed in early 2010, the large multinational acquired another company with a varicose vein device. The medical device start-up office was slowly integrated into the far larger VNUS facility, and I was promoted to plant controller of the now joint operation. It was a big promotion, and I was excited. However, I chafed somewhat under the rigid corporate controls of a multinational company. Any rigid control over my life smelled like being in the Assembly again. To this day, when someone tells me that I must do or think a certain way, my first response is to push back. I will do a certain thing or accept a thing as true only after I have sufficiently researched on my own to verify first.

Management would fly in from the corporate office once per quarter to review results. The local team would get yelled at for hours during an intense meeting where every single penny spent was scrutinized. Then, the team would go out for a very expensive dinner at one of the nicest restaurants San Jose had to offer. Going from yelling over pennies in a manufacturing cost analysis to seeing plates covered with large helpings of steak and lobster and glasses repeatedly filled with expensive alcohol was quite the juxtaposition. As it turned out, even though I was happy that I had been promoted, I ended up not being happy with the corporate culture and all of the yelling that came along with it. I soon realized that, despite talk of my potentially working overseas and the adventure that came with that experience, this was not the company for me.

Then, late one summer afternoon, I saw her.

I was walking down a hallway at the end of the day one Friday afternoon in August 2010. My plan was to do a bit more work, then go for a run on the trail behind the office (a trail upon which I had encountered bobcats more than once), and then head home. As I approached an intersection in the hallway, I looked both ways for cross traffic. To my right towards the kitchen, I saw nobody. To my left, about fifty feet down the hallway, I saw a goddess from behind walking away from me. She was walking fast and appeared to be leaving for the day. Her black leather purse was slung over her brown right arm and her keys were in that hand. Her left arm swung slightly as she walked. Long silky black hair with blond highlights streamed down her back from a tight ponytail high on the back of her head. She was quite petite and was dressed very professionally in jeans and what appeared from behind to be a conservative top. I also noticed her shapely rear as she walked. I took all of that in during the second or two that I passed through that hallway intersection.

I was smitten ... even with that brief glance from behind, she was obviously gorgeous.

As fate would have it, the next week I was called into a meeting with the R&D team to discuss the new purchase order system that the large multinational was putting in place. As I walked in, I glanced to my right and there was the gorgeous woman I had seen. I was early, so I said hello to the one person in the room that I knew, and then introduced myself to the others. Turns out her name was Chanthy (pronounced shawn-TEE). It was a Cambodian name, I learned, as she spoke to me with no accent. She spoke very intelligently and in a straightforward manner that was not in any way suggestive or flirtatious. There were other women in the office who were quite obvious flirts, both acting and dressing the part, but she was professional as could be. She had bright and intelligent almond-shaped dark brown eyes and very smooth beautiful skin with cute ears. She also had a strong chin, full shapely lips, and a button nose. The rest of her was just as amazing to look at, but as I noted before she was dressed very professionally and displayed no cleavage whatsoever. It was impossible to hide her curviness, but she shouldn't have to. During the entire meeting, she conducted herself very professionally and intelligently.

We've all worked with the typical cast of characters. Cleavage woman. Always has his shirt buttoned down a bit to show chest hair guy. Stiletto heels with miniskirt lady. Always making inappropriate slightly sexually suggestive jokes guy. Covered in six inches of makeup girl. Looks everything with two legs up and down with his eyes guy. That typical cast of characters that somehow manages to constantly walk right alongside the border of what is appropriate in the workplace and yet rarely seems to truly step over the line and actually commit a violation.

She was not one of these and neither was I.

If I was smitten before, I was absolutely done—for now. Gone were my reservations about starting to date again. Gone were any fears of what to do or say. I was ready. I had never been on a date with a truly drop-dead gorgeous woman before (a woman that, upon walking into a restaurant, almost every man would turn and look at), and I decided that would change in the near future.

As I had mentioned, I was not happy at the large multinational. The corporate management team was talking to me about career opportunities at the corporation that would open up if I did well in San Jose. However, I was essentially looking at doing the exact same cost accounting job for about a decade before being allowed to move up the ladder. That did not appeal to me at all. I really missed the excitement and constantly changing challenges of a start-up. Very gently, I began prodding my network to see if there were any opportunities. After about a month, I came across an opportunity fed to me by two of my former coworkers from the medical device start-up. It was an exciting start-up that was just getting off the ground floor and beginning market beta testing of its product. If hired, I would be getting in at a start-up at that key launch time. This was an opportunity the likes of which dreams are made of, so I jumped on it. I turned in a rather terse resignation letter to the large multinational management. Had I that to do over, I would. However, time moves on relentlessly and nothing can be changed now.

As I considered leaving, I decided to try to take something along with me. I was going to ask this incredible woman out on a date. What was the best way to do this, you ask? After not dating for about a decade and a half, I had to think about this a bit. Well, I sent her a friend request on Facebook [facepalm]. She accepted, and I started the research. Single? Check. Interested in finding someone? Check. Likes some similar things that I do? Check. Interested in trying new things that she hadn't before? Check.

I know, I'll send her a private Facebook message! [facepalm]

Jesus-H ... I mean, really? Were you that ... well, yes, as it turned out, I was.

We began exchanging a few simple messages, and they were friendly. She seemed warm, and she had already shown that she had a great sense of humor. Having said that, her sarcastic wit can be both legendary and deadly. Two rules to remember in dealing with my wife. Rule #1:

don't screw with her. Rule #2: see rule #1. After perhaps a week or two of communicating back and forth, I asked her if I could call her. She said yes. You know how monarch butterflies migrate in groups tens of thousands strong? You don't??? You should look it up. It's amazing!!! Before I made the call, a group of those butterflies tens of thousands strong took up residence in my stomach. I was so nervous I could barely see straight or think rationally. I did a quick meditation routine to become aware of my heart rate and breathing and work to slow it. The call went well. We talked for quite some time and agreed to go out to dinner, but also to keep it quiet since we still worked together. We didn't want to cause a stir, regardless of the fact that I was planning on leaving the company. Over the next few days, we talked on the phone almost every day.

Then the night of the date came. I had not been on a date like this ... just asking a woman to go out ... since my first month of college in 1995. The Assembly had essentially restricted me from any kind of dating during my entire tenure there, and then I had married in the cult. Date? I'm going on a date??? But ... I ... it's been fifteen years since my last date ... literally fifteen years!!!!!

Terror is not even close to what I felt. Self-doubt coursed through me like a river at full flood stage. What would I say? Why would she like me? Did I even know what the heck I was doing??? No idea. Excited. Nervous. Fearful. I was even fighting back the Assembly conditioning that was screaming "SINNER!!!!!" at me. I felt like a high school kid again ... afraid of the unknown and struggling to go forward.

Friday, September 10th, 2010, arrived and I had worked all week on managing my nervousness and fear.

Talking to her for a couple of hours almost every night leading up to this helped a lot since I had some foundation to base conversation on at dinner. I picked her up, and she was radiant. Gorgeous didn't even come close. Remember the conservative work attire? Not here. Full cleavage on display! We had a really nice dinner, spoke nonstop (no uncomfortable pauses in the conversation), and overall had a really nice evening at dinner and then walking in downtown San Jose. I dropped her off, and by the time we said goodnight to each other, we had already planned our next date for the following week. Yes, that is how well it went. Before we had even ended the first date, we already had the second date planned.

Having said that, despite how well it went there was one element of our first date which bears mentioning. I couldn't help but notice the looks some people gave us, and even some quietly muttered nonsense half under people's breath. You see, we were a white man and a Cambodian woman, and I couldn't help but notice that people were discriminating against us. I had always been an opponent of any type of discrimination or prejudice and a proponent of all things equality. The exception being my phobic-phobe-a-phobia regarding LGBTQ+ people during my cult tenure. However, I had never been a direct recipient of racism before that night.

As the night progressed, I began growing angry. I

didn't want to show this, so I tried to hide it. The feeling kept growing and growing. I didn't want her to think I was just some angry person or something. At some point she noticed and asked what was up. I told her what I had noticed. Then, she said something that broke my heart. Dr. Richard Dawkins talks about consciousness raising moments. Moments where one learns or experiences something, and forever after their view of the world is fundamentally altered, for better or worse. For me, this was one of those moments. She said that if I wanted to be with her, I had to get used to it. She had been called every manner of racial epithet, had been treated to the worst racist trash this country had to offer, and if I wanted to be in a relationship with her, I better get used to it because it wasn't going to just go away. My anger evaporated, but I was suddenly very sad.

Wait, this woman I was with ... this intelligent, beautiful creature ... had been treated this way so much that I just needed to get used to it? Wow. My opinion of humanity sank that night. Today, I am accustomed to the regular experience of either implicit or explicit racism when I am with her, but I'm still angered and saddened by it. Nothing can really change that.

All in all, the night remained amazing, though, and the relationship developed from there.

We continued seeing each other. We continued talking on the phone literally every single night. Deep life issues. Plans for the future. What were our goals and expectations for a long-term relationship? We talked and talked and talked. She began coming to the church that I was a part of, but she never felt welcomed. As she approached the entrance, nobody would greet her and nobody would approach to talk to her as she sat alone (I was up on stage to lead the singing) waiting for things to start. She wasn't the only one who felt that something was off at this church. The church grew for about the first year after I started attending (years before I had met her), and then that process reversed course and it began shrinking. I watched as people continued to leave and the congregation continued to shrink. There were reasons for this that are now obvious that I will get into later.

Back to Chanthy, I'd never felt so connected to someone before. We were both passionate about life and each other. The building blocks for a permanent commitment were already being laid down, but both of us were willing ourselves to take it slow. We had both been through very serious breakups pretty recently. My divorce was being finalized (including a mandatory six-month cooling-off period), and Chanthy had been in a ten-year relationship complete with engagement that had come to a very difficult end. For these reasons, we were both making sure to think things through very clearly and temper our emotions with rationality. Given how gorgeous she is, taking it slow was very difficult. We're married now, so you know we did the deed at some point.

Sheesh ... nosy much? You people, what are you thinking right now??? Oh, well, since the reader is already imagining it ...

The first time I undressed her and saw it all my heart just about stopped. A true goddess lay before me, and I (a mere mortal) wanted to have her? The curviness visible through her clothes was nothing compared to what she looked like naked. It was a wonderful encounter, and there would be (still are) many more. Today, married and with a child, we still enjoy a very active and passionate sex life.

Shortly after we became sexually intimate, she began coming up to the San Leandro house for weekends. Being a dog lover, Chanthy immediately bonded with Lucy and started bringing her little gifts when she came by. Lucy also immediately took to Chanthy and would come out front with me and wait for her to arrive every Friday. The months just flew by and winter passed into spring. Given how things were developing, we began talking about moving in together. I was quickly losing the ability to keep the home I owned in San Leandro, as well. Between the obscene Bay Area mortgage payment, the fact that the house had lost more than 50 percent of its value due to the ongoing financial crisis that began in 2008, the fact that I was making rather large payments to my ex-wife as part of the divorce deal, and the fact that my student loans for the MBA were now requiring payments ... I was just not able to make things work. The timing for us to start talking about moving in together was good. As with all things, we talked in a great deal of detail about what living together would look like. How would we do chores? How would we handle cooking responsibilities? How would we split the costs of rent, utilities, etc.? We had all of the practical conversations *prior* to making a decision to move in together.

From our research into relationship issues and conversations with our therapist, we've discovered that this is actually quite rare. Much of the research we've read suggests strongly that one of the primary reasons for divorce (and other long-term relationship failure) is that people *do not have* these conversations. They move in based on assumptions about how it is going to work, rather than having discussions about what to realistically expect. Since assumptions are made, expectations are not met, and relationships fracture and end. This tendency has been referred to as "sliding into decisions." We've been dating for a long time, so we may as well move in. We've been living together for a long time, so we may as well get married. We're married, so we may as well have a child. Failure to actually have the real conversations about the day to day, and a slide into a new situation rather than a planned move. We determined that we would always communicate about the practical matters of the relationship. We don't always do it perfectly (who does?), but we at all times put in the good faith effort to make sure we understand one another's needs, expectations, and feelings.

During this time, I also separated myself from the church I had been attending. As discussed, the congregation had just continued shrinking and it reached a point where I recognized what was happening. The church wasn't going to make it. I had already been in that place in the past and the honest reason why it did not succeed in my opinion was that the pastor was a bit of an authoritarian. Despite the way I had healed in that church through the pastor's constant preaching about grace, upon hearing suggestions about how we could change or improve things, he would say things like, "Our form of church government is *not* a democracy." Really? What was it then??? If it wasn't a democracy, what type of autocratic regime were we living in? I believe he was carrying his own baggage from the fundamentalist upbringing he had but wasn't really dealing with it or acknowledging how it was still burdening him.

As I said, the time had come for me to move on. Chanthy and I continued our faith journey. We prayed together before every meal. We prayed when we went to sleep and when we woke. We had items and sayings of faith around the home. It seemed we would continue a journey of faith, but we were now discovering together what that would mean. A part of what it would mean is that we would not continue attending that church. From the beginning we had always communicated about important things, and now we communicated about where we would go in this journey as well.

She had made it quite clear that she did not feel safe in that San Leandro neighborhood, and how could I blame her? I had never felt safe there. Emergency sirens, as I previously mentioned, were as common as the banshee wail of the BART trains. In late 2011, I secured a short sale on the house. As mentioned earlier, my financial situation had simply become untenable. I would not make any money, but although it was technically considered a short sale, I prevented the bank from taking a loss. Between the interest I had paid in over the years, and the sale value, the total was quite a bit more than the original principal balance of the loan. That gave me a lot of peace about the transaction.

We moved into an apartment in south San Jose. The Palm Valley Apartments accepted dogs, which meant I could bring Lucy. Moving in was easy as neither of us had much in the way of furniture or other belongings beyond clothes. We began doing couple's shopping like looking for inexpensive but reasonable quality couches, dining table, etc. and settled in together. We also began attending a few churches to see if we could find a home for our faith where we would both feel a sense of welcome and belonging.

Life was really, really good. Honestly, I had not been this happy since childhood. At right is a picture of us taken during this time period at South Lake, elevation 9,700 feet, near my hometown of Bishop. The winter prior had been very snowy and even in early July when this was taken there were significant snowfields up in the high country.

From late 2011 and into 2012, we continued to deepen our love for one another and talked about starting a family together. There were challenges. We didn't always agree about everything, but we loved each other deeply and it showed in everything we did together. In September 2012, I gave Chanthy a big hint as to how serious I was about her. We had our greyhound, Lucy, but she had always talked about having a little dog like a chihuahua. Then one day I was doing some research and I found a 2.2lbs chihuahua puppy at the animal shelter. She was marked like a Doberman in color. Her name was Carly. I told Chanthy we were going out to run some errands and that I really wanted her to come. I don't think she realized what we were doing until we arrived at the shelter. There, in a rather small cage (that strangely seemed huge around this tiny canine form), was Carly. We fell in love. She became ours. Worms infested her gut so badly that you could see them writhing in her belly through her skin, but we fixed that. She grew. She climbed all over Lucy (who took it with the patience of Job). Now at nine years old she is still with us and has been an amazing addition to our family.

Then, since we had been talking about what our future held, I suggested that we head to Shane Company to look at engagement sets. Not that we would become engaged any time soon, I said, but that we would just get an idea for pricing. As I mentioned before, we talked about and planned for everything. While there, she showed me what kind of thing she would want, and to her genuine surprise I bought it and proposed. She agreed to become Mrs. Chanthy Thai Conger, and I agreed to love and cherish her above all others to the end of our days. We went home so happy, and so hopeful for our future. We would not begin trying for a baby right away ... we would be married first. Therefore, one of the direct purposes of getting married, aside from wanting to share our love for one another until the end of our lives, was in order to start a family. In the past, as discussed, she had been engaged for nearly ten years. She was therefore very sensitive about the length of the engagement and asked when I thought the wedding would come. It was a test of how serious I was.

One year in the future?
Two years?
Five years?

She was serious ... she was expecting a very long-term engagement. Since we had talked about things, I was surprised by her expectations, but those were based on her history and not on our conversations. I very pleasantly surprised her by saying quite firmly that we should be engaged for no less than six months, but no more than one year. What did she think? The look on her face said it all. She was thrilled! I was taking this seriously, and the proposal was not just trying to soothe her or quiet her down while we just kept on keeping on. We talked wedding plans. We talked honeymoon spots. We began looking at dates that would capture the best of both of these events. On the previous page is a photo of us from our engagement shoot. Carly the wonder-huahua is on Chanthy's lap. NOTE: during this shoot I had a horrible flu and felt like I was dying. We are both surprised our photos turned out so well given how horribly sick I was.

In the end, we decided to marry in the month of May 2013. This would hopefully provide great weather in the San Francisco Bay Area and also allow us great weather in our chosen honeymoon destination of Costa Rica. Costa Rica's dry season lasts from mid-January to mid-May, so we would be flying down (hopefully) during the last of the good weather before the tropical rainy season arrived. We prayed, we thanked God for our blessings, we planned for the greatest event in either of our lives. Our wedding (we decided) would take place on a Hornblower Cruise of San Francisco Bay. Our honeymoon would be in Costa Rica—two nights at the Arenal Nayara near the famous volcano, and a few more nights at the beach resort Westin Playa Conchal.

Excitement ... we were so thrilled!

At this point, reflecting on the vast differences between the natural healthy evolution of my relationship with Chanthy versus what now seems to be the very mechanical and forced way I came together with my ex-wife is important. Chanthy and I naturally fell for one another. I now understood what it meant to simply allow one's heart to move. To allow one's heart to love. None of the "God told me to" or "the leadership thinks it's great" or "I need permission from someone even though I am a grown adult." Just love, grow, deepen, and move. The contrast could not have been more stark, and illustrated just how deeply controlled I was back in the cult days.

During this time, my current company also began its IPO push. I was so busy. However, I had been busier before. Given the overall joy flowing through my life, this workload was nothing. Audit requests came in with such frenzy that I was confused as to how to even start. I was running reports, then more reports, then after those reports I was scanning invoices and bills. I was still the only accountant for the company, so everything came back to me. It was crazy. However, there was hope both for me personally and for the company professionally. I was literally answering audit requests from the honeymoon (at this point enter scene of my wife telling me in no uncertain terms that it was time to put away the laptop so we could head to the beach). I poured hours beyond count into the IPO, but I had my rock ... Chanthy ... standing beside me. The CEO and others involved graciously gave me the space for my moment in the sun (wedding and honeymoon), and then it was back to work when we returned.

The founders of my current company were beyond supportive of us during this time, as were the CEO of the company and his wife. Special thanks to them for their kindness and support over the years.

It was a magical day. She was radiant. The plan was to sail past Alcatraz, go out to the Golden Gate, pass the various San Francisco city tourist spots, and then return to Berkeley where we launched. However, the wind came up and things changed. We hit Alcatraz, toured some city spots, rounded Treasure Island, and then returned to port. The wind hit Chanthy hard and blew away her wedding veil never to be recovered, but we had a good time and laughed it off. Hard waves hit the ship at one point, even breaking glasses in the bar, but it all worked out. It was a magical day ... and wedding night. The next morning, we had breakfast with a large group of family who had attended the wedding and returned to our apartment. We had dropped off our precious canine family at the kennel the day before, so our apartment seemed empty the night after our wedding. However, the next morning we boarded a plane for Costa Rica.

The trip was ... long. San Jose to Houston, and a layover of a couple of hours. We arrived in Costa Rica after the sun had set, and then we were picked up by our shuttle driver. Four hours later, at about midnight local time, we arrived at our first destination. The room was covered in rose petals and there were towels shaped into swans on the bed. After that long trip, the reception was amazing.

What a magical time it was.

We saw wild toucans and sloths. We rode horseback

through a river near the Arenal Volcano. We drove through hundreds of miles of rainforest, dry forest, plains, and to the seashore. One of my wife's coworkers, upon her return and commenting on the Facebook photos, said, "That was a badassed honeymoon!" We had a clear and unrestricted view of Arenal Volcano out of our bungalow, which we heard repeatedly is a very rare sight given how much rain normally falls there. The beach at Playa Conchal was amazing, both because nobody was on it and because the water temperature was so perfect. Sitting on that beach watching small lazy waves come in relaxed us beyond measure. We saw rays swim beneath a jet ski we were riding. We say howler monkeys in the trees. We saw toucans flying in the wild. We snorkeled with tropical fish and watched the sun set from a ship at sea. It was amazing, and neither of us will forget it.

One afternoon at the Westin Playa Conchal, a tropical rainstorm moved in. We decided to go for a walk on the beach in the rain. It turns out, this was something of a dream idea for my wife. The rain was warm, and we wandered down the beach in bikini and swim trunks having the time of our lives. As the storm moved off, we got some great photos. We want to go back someday with our son.

Upon returning from that trip we continued to plan for our future. Not much changed about our actual home life. We had been living together for seventeen months, we still had our two dogs to care for, and we loved them. We discovered that (as I had long suspected) the large multinational was indeed planning on closing the facility where Chanthy worked and our discussions shifted to what we would do after she worked her last day there. Since I was working from home, we could conceivably leave the expensive Bay Area and move out closer to the Sierra foothills. We would be able to rent a much larger place for far less money and be closer to the wild spaces including the hiking/camping/fishing/skiing that we both enjoyed. At the end of the day, after much discussion, we decided we would try to find a place to rent somewhere outside of Sacramento.

Also upon our return, we decided to put our plan for having children into place and start actively working towards that goal. Before I met Chanthy, but after leaving the Assembly, I had an annual tradition of floating the Owens River near my hometown of Bishop with my old friend Danny, and Chanthy had joined us in the tradition since I began dating her. That year, we floated along and kept to ourselves the knowledge that she had stopped taking her contraceptive medication that very holiday. Only we knew that the July 4th holiday in 2013 marked the beginning of our attempts to start a family. In the spirit of family planning, we purchased a few items that would come in handy for a baby up to and including a family SUV.

What neither of us knew was years of pain and anguish lay before us as we repeatedly tried and failed to have a child, and that with the deaths of all of those children, our faith would also die.

Chapter Seven
An End of Faith

This chapter will involve some rather detailed discussion surrounding our sexuality and the overall reproductive process. Not a disclaimer, but I don't want the reader to be surprised. The reason for this is because I would really like this chapter to be a help to anyone else suffering through infertility. If you have struggled, or are struggling, with infertility, it is the hope of both my wife and I that this chapter will help you to navigate this difficult process.

Like so many other couples, we thought having children would be easy. Marry, have some passionate and steamy sex, and PRESTO! Pregnancy would come easily, of course, with no struggle or delay. We always had (and still have) a very active and passionate sex life, so we just kept on with our usual bedroom (and other rooms in the home) habits. On average, we had stabilized from the super passionate sex life of a newly forged couple, where we might have sex twice a day, and scaled back naturally to sex on average every two to three days. We still enjoy that frequency very much, I am quite happy to say.

Since Chanthy is so smoking hot, getting in the mood takes no effort at all.

After a few months without conceiving, we started doing some research on how to help the process along. We dropped alcohol almost completely from our diet to start, agreeing that we would only have it on special occasions. Another change was to start timing her ovulation cycles to increase our chances of conception. We would have sex three or four days in a row, starting the day before we thought she would ovulate. Still, we were unable to conceive.

At the same time, we continued looking for a place to rent in the greater Sacramento area. Eventually, we found a great little house in a quiet neighborhood on the south side of Elk Grove, California. It was a 1,749-square foot house with a decent backyard and a large park right down the street (easy walking distance). We would pay $1,799/month for this house. Now, compare that to the $2,799/month we were paying for a 1,000-square foot apartment in San Jose and the reader will understand our desire to move. The frenetic pace of activity in the San Francisco Bay Area was behind us. Now, we would live in a much quieter neighborhood with a slower pace to life and a much lower cost of living. The reduced stress, we thought, would also help us to conceive. Kirkwood Ski Resort was an easy ninety minutes away when the roads were clear. Silver Lake, a great fishing spot near Kirkwood, became a favorite of ours.

December 3rd, 2013, was Chanthy's last day at the large multinational. We had started slowly moving items to our rental home in Elk Grove in mid-November, so we were very prepared to move in the days immediately after her layoff. She received a rather generous severance package and decided to switch careers. Rather than looking for a new job, she decided she wanted to be a full-time mom. Since we were actively trying to have a baby, we reasoned that it made no sense for her to find a job, and possibly go out on maternity leave a few months later, never to return to work. It would be rough for her to learn a new position, and then just leave it. Also, it would be *very* unfair to a potential employer to invest the time in training only to lose the person they just hired. Chanthy and I both feel a pretty profound level of professional responsibility. We just can't leave things hanging and always feel that we need to do everything in our ability to go above and beyond the call of duty. She knew that it would be very hard for her, emotionally, to just leave a new employer like that.

After the move, we settled into our new place and she began adding mindfulness meditations to her routine, seeking to calm herself and remove stresses that could be inhibiting pregnancy. We also did some nesting in the hopes that we would be welcoming home our baby soon. Finally, we began attending some local churches to see if we could find a home for the faith we continued to embrace together. One church we went to very near our Elk Grove rental was *very* diverse. We both felt very much at home there and began attending. However, our continued struggles to become pregnant were weighing on us.

As 2014 progressed, we began seriously looking into fertility treatments. Our initial testing showed all clear. Nothing appeared to be outwardly wrong with either of us physically, but pregnancy continued to elude us. Our first decision was to try two intrauterine insemination (IUI) treatments. In this procedure, the clinic would collect a sperm sample from me and deposit it directly into my wife's uterus during the peak ovulation window. She would also be on medications to overstimulate her body's natural ovulation processes in the hopes of producing more than one ovum. This would maximize the potential for Chanthy to become pregnant. We did this two days in a row, and then waited.

The procedure failed. We went through another IUI a few months later, which also failed. Heartbreak. These treatments are relatively inexpensive. Ours, including meds, were about $2,500/procedure. Due to the relative cost, this procedure is the first choice for most couples suffering through infertility.

At this point, we also realized something that further broke our hearts. The first IUI passed in such a way that Chanthy's monthly cycle was not in any way interrupted, delayed, or anything. Then after the second one, her period was about two weeks late and much heavier than usual.

This second IUI cycle clearly resulted in a miscarriage at a very early stage.

Throughout our relationship, Chanthy had always been exceedingly regular in her cycles. After we started actively trying to have children, there had been more than a couple of cycles where she was late and bled more heavily than normal. After this second IUI, where the fertility clinic was monitoring us and able to tell us what was happening, we realized that in all likelihood those cycles where she was late and had a heavier than normal bleed were also miscarriages.

Heartbroken is the appropriate word, but somehow doesn't do justice to how we felt. We stopped visiting churches, as well as stopping almost all social interaction, period, because we were depressed and just didn't want to see anyone. Seeing happy families was particularly difficult since we feared we might never have one of our own.

It seemed something might be wrong at the DNA level. One or both of us was likely delivering genetically abnormal DNA into the mix. Fertility clinics tend to assign the source of the genetic problem to the female in the majority of cases. Why? Well, there is actually a biological reason, but at this point both Chanthy and I feel that clinics in general reach this conclusion far too quickly. The real medical reason why this conclusion is the default is as follows. Males continually produce sperm in their testes throughout their lives. Every day new sperm is manufactured, and every day older sperm is reabsorbed into the male's body or ejaculated. For females, this is not the case. At the moment of a female's birth, the ovaries contain literally all of the ova they will carry for their entire life.

At birth.

There is no ova production later in life. So, if a female is trying to conceive at age twenty, then the ova are twenty years old at that point. If the female is trying to conceive at age forty, the ova are literally twice as old as they were at age twenty. This introduces the possibility that genetic degradation could have taken place over the term of the female's life, and the longer the life spent prior to attempting to have a baby, the more potential for genetic degradation there is. This is the real biologically driven reason that fertility clinics tend to assume that the female is the driving force behind any potential genetic problems. While a male is producing fresh sperm at all times through life, the female has 100 percent of her ova present in her body at birth and *never* produces any more.

In consultation with the fertility clinic, we decided to pursue an in vitro fertilization (IVF) procedure. This procedure is very different from IUI and can be upwards of ten times the cost. Instead of delivering my sperm directly into Chanthy's uterus while using medication to stimulate her ovulation, the process would be much more invasive. The IUI ovulation meds were all oral. No injections necessary; Chanthy just took some pills in the days leading up to the procedure. Not this time. Now, I would be delivering injections to her three times a day (literally morning, noon, and night), and there would be two or three injections at a time in order to boost her ovulation and hopefully produce ten to twenty ova for harvest at the fertility clinic. At the height of the process I would be delivering eight injections per day into her body.

Did I mention I have a deep phobia of needles? Yeah, I do ... to the point that I nearly pass out every time I need a shot.

Delivering those shots to her was horrifically difficult for me. It was even more difficult for her. At 4'11" tall, she had been plus or minus one hundred pounds since I had met her, and she now began gaining weight slowly but steadily due to the hormones. There was the pain of the injection itself, which in many cases needed to be delivered deep into her muscles in her stomach and buttocks, not just into the surface of the arm or shoulder. Also, the hormones affected her deeply on an emotional level. She was often just not herself. Finally, as the hormone levels built in her body over the couple of weeks the injections were to be delivered ahead of her ovulation, she began experiencing dizziness, shortness of breath, memory lapses, and a host of other physiological symptoms. I hated seeing her suffer that way, and I was dealing with panic attacks because I had to handle needles and deliver shots to her multiple times every day. One kicker to boot, the effects of the hormone boosting would last for months afterwards and affect every aspect of her character for extended periods of time.

On the day of the procedure, they put her under a local anesthetic and harvested the stimulated ova directly from her ovaries. Using ultrasound and needles to pierce her abdomen, the staff at the clinic would draw them out. While she was in the procedure, I would provide a sperm sample. The clinic would then take the harvested ova and sperm and attempt to conduct a fertilization in a petri dish. During this cycle they were able to harvest nine eggs, but only eight were successfully fertilized. After five days of developing in a petri dish, only two were healthy enough to be implanted in Chanthy's uterus. There would be none to freeze for another cycle. However, we had decided to send them away for genetic testing just to be sure they were healthy. The results came back that they were both genetically abnormal. This was extremely disappointing because it meant there was nothing left for us to implant. All that time, those injections ... nothing. It was a completely busted cycle. However, we were spared the horror of miscarriage because of this test. Also, at this point it became quite clear that one or both of us had some genetic problem going on. We just didn't know which one of us it was and the clinic continued assuming it was Chanthy. Thus, she also had the burden of guilt associated with believing that the problem was her. Through all of this, we continued to pray to the God we felt was sure to bless a responsible couple with a child, but to no avail.

It was during this time period that our beloved greyhound, Lucy, passed. She was young for the breed, only nine, and they usually live to be twelve. Cancer was the cause. We struggled with the reality that everything around us seemed to be dying. Grieving the death of our children, and now our dog, too. She was wonderful and we often have moments where we still think of her.

After spending about six months recovering, both emotionally and physically, we pursued a second more aggressive and expensive IVF procedure. The medical stimulation would be far more aggressive. Painfully, we started up the process described above again. Needles, fear, pain, waiting. During this period, due to the higher level of meds, Chanthy became *very* overstimulated. She was short of breath, dizzy, extremely bloated ... we rushed into the clinic for an evaluation, and they stepped us back on the dosage.

She was severely overstimulated, and that can cause major problems.

Finally, the day arrived to collect ova and provide the sperm sample. This time was much better, with sixteen ova collected *and* all sixteen successfully fertilized. We were very hopeful, but those hopes fell as we went on. Of the sixteen collected, only two made it. On the fifth day after ova collection, we went in and the clinic implanted both of the two seemingly healthy embryos into Chanthy.

Now, we waited for the pregnancy test to be done a few days later.

It worked!

I mean, holy-fucking-shit it actually worked! She was *pregnant*!!!

I continued the post-procedure injections for her twice per day, and she was exhibiting signs of pregnancy ranging from tender and slightly swollen breasts to slight bloating and continued slow weight gain. We went in for our first ultrasound at four weeks (because with fertility treatments they know one is supposed to be pregnant, ultrasounds begin very early) and things looked good. Although only one of the two blastocysts attached to her uterus, the embryo looked good physically. We were so excited, thinking that our nightmare was over. At the six-week visit, things were OK, but there was a concern. The baby's heart rate was just slightly slow. The clinic upped her dosage on the post-procedure hormone injections to attempt to concentrate the chemicals and strengthen the pregnancy. At about week seven, Chanthy's pregnancy symptoms completely evaporated. Just, full stop one morning when she woke up. Then we went in for our week eight ultrasound and received the devastating news that the baby had died. We were told to expect a miscarriage. Three days later it happened. It was very difficult to watch my wife go through it, and we were very emotionally compromised. Anger, depression, fear ... everything mixed together into a mash of nuclear emotional fallout.

This was far worse than the previous cycle, emotionally and physically.

The day after the ultrasound appointment when we were told to expect the miscarriage, but before it actually happened, my cousin was throwing a huge birthday party for his wife. We debated whether or not to attend because, as the reader can imagine, we really didn't feel like doing anything at all. In the end we decided to go so we could just get out of the house. We probably weren't very good company. We just sat in the same place kinda being there. Other members of my family were also at the party, so we spent the time talking to them, and my aunt and uncle and cousins of course came over to chat. None of them knew what we were going through. We just sat there kinda talking, probably more than a little dispassionately or coldly, and then left the party early.

In general, this is what we were like socially a lot of the time. On the rare occasions that we actually wanted to see people, we were really only half present, and possibly more than a little cold and dispassionate about basically everything.

We prayed, we cried, we wondered why this had to happen to us. Why, did it seem, that we were reading news stories about drug addicts abandoning their newborns in dumpsters, but God wouldn't give us a child? The Bible says he is the author of life ... why would he author life to a drug-addled addict but not to a financially successful and loving couple? We really began questioning this. If an adoption agency allowed a known drug addict to take custody of a child, but refused a responsible couple, wouldn't that agency be deemed grossly unethical? Isn't that the same as what God was doing? Why wasn't He deemed grossly unethical? Why wasn't he held to the same standard that we would hold an adoption agency to? We had stopped even looking for a good church months before, but our doubts continued to grow as we went through this agony. Day by day, week by week, and month by month ... the foundation of our faith was being worn away like the storm surge of a hurricane wearing away the foundation of a beach house.

After spending some months recovering we evaluated our options for continuing our journey to start a family. We had the financial resources to do at most two more IVF cycles before our credit would be stretched to the max. Considering all that was said by our current clinic, we determined that in all likelihood it was Chanthy that had the genetic problems (the reader can reference the reasons why medical professionals take this position from an earlier paragraph). As a result, we decided to do an IVF cycle with donor eggs. The baby would be genetically mine, but not genetically Chanthy's. She would carry the baby, birth the baby, nurture and raise, but the DNA would not be hers. At this point, we were totally OK with this since just having a child at all seemed so far out of reach.

However, that last IVF turned out to be the worst one by far.

Not only had we spent over $40,000 on a highly specialized IVF procedure with a world-renowned expert, but we had been required to travel a few hundred miles to the doctor's office to do so. Not only had that procedure not gone well, but the results were so abysmal that we literally had one viable embryo to implant. Then ... everything seemed to look better! My wife exhibited symptoms of pregnancy almost right away. We went in for our first ultrasound at four weeks and the baby looked great! Heart rate strong, morphology looking good, wife's vitals all well into the green. Our hopes rose!!! Two weeks later was our second ultrasound and again everything looked fantastic. Baby showed solid growth, strong heart rate, good morphology ... again, our hopes rose!!! The appointments every two weeks passed until week twelve, right at the end of the first trimester, and things took a bad turn. My wife's pregnancy symptoms simply stopped one day. Cold stop. At the next ultrasound our whole world once again crumbled to ruin.

Our baby was dead.

Again ...

After all of the positive vitals in the previous appointments, all of the hopes raised up, all of the positive ultrasounds and measurements of vital signs ... the tragic death of our child was once again the end result.

That wasn't the worst of it, either ...

We were told to expect a miscarriage any day and had been through this before, with my wife going through the incredibly painful experience (both physically and emotionally) after the previous IVF. The waiting started ... and we waited ... and waited ... and then continued to wait. After over a week, we contacted her gynecologist and told her about what was going on and asked for advice. She knew we were getting fertility treatments, but we filled her in on the specific details of our current situation. She recommended that we schedule a surgical procedure to remove our dead child from my wife's womb. You see, since her body was not proceeding with the miscarriage naturally, there was great risk to her long-term health, and even her very life, if we did nothing.

Surgery? Not only had we lost another baby, but ... *surgery*??? For fuck's sake, WHAT THE HELL??????????

To add insult to injury, we discovered something further *after* the cycle failed. The world-renowned specialist we had seen recommended that I have a sperm DNA fragmentation test done. This would test the genetic content of my sperm for problems. Wait, you waited until *after* the procedure to recommend this? None of the other clinics had even recommended it at all??? I had the test done. Turns out, Chanthy is not the problem genetically.

It's me.

Ninety-five percent of my sperm has abnormal DNA. What the fuck are the chances that any IUI or IVF procedure would work for us if 95 percent of my DNA is abnormal??? Nobody recommended this fucking test earlier??????????

We have been asked by other couples what our advice is if infertility is something that comes up in their lives. The first piece of advice we give is always the same ... the male needs to order a sperm DNA fragmentation test as the absolute first hurdle. It costs a few thousand dollars, but if the results are bad, it could save tens of thousands more in further fertility treatments.

In total, we spent just over $89,000 on fertility treatments. The sperm DNA fragmentation test cost us $3,500. We could have saved ... [choke] ... nearly $86,000 if that DNA test was the first thing we had done. In all likelihood, if we had elected a procedure with donor sperm rather than donor ova, Chanthy would have not only become pregnant but carried to full term. This explained why every single cycle had resulted in just a couple of embryos that the clinics could implant in my wife. Not only that, it explained why embryos would survive a few weeks and then die. There are many genetic conditions that do not prevent pregnancy, they just prevent it from going to full term. No matter the source of the ova, 95 percent of the sperm contained bad DNA. Carrying a pregnancy to term with my DNA was nearly guaranteed not to happen.

This was a very tough pill for me to swallow. It meant I was nearly guaranteed never to have a child that was biologically mine. I was really shaken by this news. Nobody expects something like this. We received this information just a day or two before the procedure to surgically remove our dead child from my wife. On the day of the procedure, we really didn't talk much. I sat in the waiting room praying, with my pocket Bible in my hand reading in between prayers. "Oh Lord, guide the hands of the doctor and her team so my wife comes through this successfully," and other such things.

Mid-prayer, my eyes popped open. I slowly looked around. Upon realizing I was the only one in the room (even the receptionist had stepped away from her window), I said out loud to nobody in particular, "If my wife comes through this surgery OK, it will not be because of any god. It will be due to the skill of the doctor and her team." It was on this day that I realized my faith had died. It had actually died sometime in the past, but I hadn't even been aware of it. I had continued my prayers, Bible devotions, and other religious activities because I had belief in faith itself, not because I believed in any god.

My faith was dead. I was an atheist.

Placing my Bible back into my pocket, I sat quietly and waited. I didn't say anything to Chanthy about this for about a week. We cried a lot after that procedure. The embryonic tissue was sent away for analysis and the results were not surprising. The child was genetically abnormal. One day about a week later, I took a break from work and found that Chanthy was sitting at the dining room table with a vacant expression on her face. I sat down next to her, we kissed, and I put my arm around her as she cried on my shoulder and my tears fell into that long silky black hair. I said, "I have something to tell you."

She quietly said, "What?"

"I'm an atheist. I've been doubting for a long time, and I've finally reached the conclusion that there simply can't be a good and loving god ruling over the universe. It just makes no sense to me anymore."

She looked at me with a completely flat expression for a moment and then said, "I agree."

Without another word, we both rose and removed every single religious symbol from our home. Crosses, the Serenity Prayer ... everything. I decided to keep all of my various Bibles and religious books because they were a very important part of my personal history and the evolution of who I am as a person. It felt good, actually, to be doing something. Once we had all of our religious symbology down, we went shopping. There was empty space on the walls, on shelves, and elsewhere. We decided to slowly fill it and we began that very day.

At the end of the day, there were three deaths resulting from that final IVF cycle. Not only the death of our baby, but the death of my faith and Chanthy's faith as well. The journey to this place of realization was long and difficult. We had suffered more miscarriages than either of us wanted to count, and our beloved greyhound (Lucy) had died of cancer at a young age. There had also been no shortage of in-law drama as we suffered through everything, in no small part due to the fact that we just weren't good company when we saw people. We had spent over $89,000, and in the end we felt like everything died. It was time to take a big step back, take a good look at the big picture, and start rethinking where we were going.

Chapter Eight
Atheism

There is actually a lot of confusion in the general public on the topic of atheism. This chapter is intended to clear up some of that confusion, and simultaneously walk through how my thinking changed in the years after leaving the cult.

First off, atheism is not an "ism." Isms come with worldviews. Capitalism. Fascism. Communism. Socialism. Catholicism. All of these come with a view of how the world best works. The atheist view comes with no comment on how the world works, how best it works, how society should order itself ... nothing like that. A view that many atheists hold that *is* an ism would be secular humanism. This comes with a worldview. Atheism, however, is a simple one-word answer to a very direct question.

The Question: Do you believe there is a god?
The Answer: No.

No, there is not insufficient evidence to reach that conclusion. Not, "I absolutely believe there is not a god." No, not that. Nor, "I can definitively prove that there is no god." Simply that one does not believe that there is a god unless sufficient evidence is provided to justify that conclusion. Why, then, don't you call yourself an agnostic?

Simple, I *am* an agnostic, and I am also an atheist. The two are not mutually exclusive. I do not believe that there is sufficient evidence to come to the conclusion that there is a god. I *do not* know for sure that is the case. Check out the simple chart below for a visual of what I'm talking about.

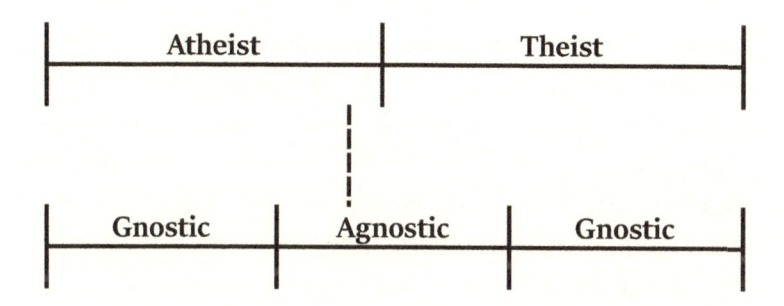

Atheist	Theist
Gnostic	Agnostic	Gnostic

As displayed on the chart above, because I don't actively believe there *is* a god, I am an atheist. I am simply an agnostic atheist because I don't know for sure. The dashed vertical line is where I would fall on the chart. There are also agnostic theists ... those who believe in a god, but do not know for sure and would never try to prove it to anyone or otherwise make converts. There are gnostic or "hard" atheists who do definitely claim they can prove that there is no god, but they are in the minority. The majority of atheists, even well-known ones, are agnostic about it. They simply refute the definitive claim that there is a god. They don't prove that there is not one, they reject the idea that there is one. Finally, there are gnostic theists ... those who definitively believe there is a god and believe they can prove it.

Perhaps a good analogy that will help can come from my profession in the Silicon Valley medical device and biotech industry. If I have a drug and I claim that I can cure cancer with it, it is *not* the job of other people or regulatory authorities like the Food & Drug Administration (FDA) to prove that my claim is *wrong*. It is my job to prove the claim is *true*. I must, through objectively verifiable clinical evidence, demonstrate that my drug cures cancer, and I must do so *prior* to marketing it to anyone. The FDA is agnostic about it. They don't have a position that my drug *does not* cure cancer. They are simply withholding support of that claim until such time as I can prove it. This is the same with the position of most atheists. We aren't claiming that there definitively is no god. We are simply withholding belief until such time as there is objectively verifiable evidence to prove it.

You see, evangelical fundamentalists claim that their god is a cure for cancer (that is, if he so chooses to be). Not only that, but their god is also a panacea ... a cure-all for every condition known to humanity even to the point of curing the fatal flaw in your immortal soul. They ask you to believe what they say, upon pain of eternal torture in the fires of hell below, and they provide you no evidence that this cure-all even exists. That, to me, is the galling part of it. In the case of the cancer drug, I can actually *show you* the drug. Here it is ... it's in this vial, right here. I simply need to prove that it actually cures cancer. With the god claim, they can't even show you the god, much less prove that it is a cure for anything.

Hopefully this analogy clears things up with the atheist versus agnostic false dichotomy. They are not mutually exclusive, and most atheists are actually also agnostic about it at the same time. There are also agnostic theists—those who believe but simultaneously do not definitively state that it must be true. As an atheist, I am not claiming with absolute certainty that there is no god. I am simply waiting for objectively verifiable evidence that a god exists before I believe, in the same way that I would wait for a company to *prove* they can cure cancer before I believe it.

Despite the trauma leading up to our realization that we were atheists, there was much more that went into this stage of our personal evolution. Chanthy will, in her own way and in her own time, speak to the significant steps on her own journey. Here is a summary of the other steps, along with mine.

My faith began unraveling like the peeling back of the layers of an onion beginning with the realization discussed in an earlier chapter where I had recognized a delusion. If the Bible says in 1 Corinthians 5 that we should not even eat a meal with a sexually perverse individual, then how could god have called me to fervently support such a person as George Geftakys? The cognitive dissonance there was just too much. After that realization I began evaluating other ideas that I had been taught in the cult and held dear for years. This evaluation took many years and spanned the time of many of the life events discussed up to this point in the book.

Funny thing about onions and their layers. The outside is the hardest, and yet the most fragile. It is so easy to fracture. Yet, when one tries to remove it piece by piece, it is not so easy. Sometimes, one begins peeling and a tiny flake comes off. Sometimes a huge portion comes off all at once. It takes a bit of work, but eventually it all comes free, revealing the second layer. The second layer is simultaneously tougher and yet more pliable at the same time, but once it is worked free it comes off in larger chunks ... often all in one pull as one gently peels away the entire layer in one go. After that, the layers are pretty uniform. My faith experience was much like this as I evolved post-Assembly and began to peel back all those various onion layers. The early layers took a lot of time and came away in small pieces, but once it began, the later layers began coming apart quickly.

Evolution ... the scientific evidence to support the validity of this working theory is beyond overwhelming. Seriously, we understand how evolution works *better* than we understand gravity. Simply search "unified theory of physics" to understand what I mean or read Stephen Hawking's books *A Brief History of Time* and *The Universe in a Nutshell*.

LGBTQ+ ... be who you are. The evidence is overwhelming that this is not a lifestyle choice, but a matter of one's biological neurology at birth.

Literal Bible ... not so much. Biblical inerrancy is a concept that simply can't stand after an evaluation of the available evidence. There are ideas put forth in the Bible that are patently false from a scientific perspective. Examples: bats are not birds and whales are not fish. There are also morally abhorrent portions of scripture that one would think were written about some twentieth-century dictator, not about a perfect or loving god. More on this shortly.

Everything I had held dear for nearly a decade fell under the microscope. It has been said by many that the best way to make an atheist out of someone is to ask them to actually sit down and read the Bible from the first verse of Genesis straight through to the last verse of Revelation. I'm not sure I agree. This idea might hold true for a more liberal believer that hadn't actually read the Bible for themselves, but not for someone in a cult like I was. I had read the Bible from beginning to end ... multiple times ... and yet I still believed. Clearly, reading alone will not make someone an atheist otherwise I would have stopped believing in 1995.

Seth Andrews from The Thinking Atheist calls the Bible, "The Goat-Herder's Guide to the Galaxy." I can't help but laugh out loud because it is absolutely appropriate. The ideas in this book are so backwards that they can't possibly be from a perfect creator of everything. However, I took a different step first, since I was still a pretty ardent believer and I had already read through the entire Bible from start to finish multiple times.

Another way to make an atheist out of someone (which I think is far more effective) is to study two things that often go hand in hand. First, study how the Bible as we know it today came to be. Who chose the books that became "inspired canon"? Why were those books chosen? Is the average Christian even aware that there are actually multiple different versions of what is considered canon depending on which particular Christian sect one is looking at? Second, study how Bible translation is actually done. The first will show you the politics at play in deciding which books were to be included in canon. The second will show you how unreliable the book you hold in your hand is. Since I had already read the Bible multiple times, I started with the first above.

Having said that, I want to take a moment to discuss a few problem passages in the Bible that often drive people towards atheism. These passages, and many others like them, are why some people say that the easiest way to create atheists is to ask people to actually read the book.

There is a common argument put forth by apologists that while there are atrocities in the Bible they are just there as a matter of recording a history. These atrocities are not condoned or advocated by Almighty God, they say, but rather they are recorded merely to show the historical events taking place during biblical history. This is patently false. There are indeed examples of this type of historical record, but there are many passages where the god of the Bible not only stamps his seal of approval on something heinous, but directly commands it. What follows are some examples. I will use biblical names in the narratives, but they are not references to any specific biblical character.

Slavery in the Bible

Jeremiah was an honest man. He had spent his life working hard to earn his way, not asking for handouts. As a farmer, his life depended deeply upon the regular arrival of the rains. The previous year, rain had not come in sufficient quantities to support his crops. He had weathered that first year of drought well enough, but when a second year of drought came, he was forced to take a loan from his wealthy neighbor to survive. The terms of the loan were pretty harsh, but so long as the rains arrived the next year, he would have been fine. The rains did not come that third year and Jeremiah defaulted on the loan. His wealthy neighbor, Jehoiachin, then presented him with an ultimatum ... become his slave for a period of six years to go free in the seventh year (including allowing Jehoiachin to use his farmland for the same time period) or be imprisoned and lose everything. After the six years were up, he would receive his land back and be able to live on his own again with a clean slate.

Jeremiah, at his wits' end, agreed to become the slave of Jehoiachin. He simply saw no other option. As a slave, he moved into the quarters occupied by the other slaves, lived off of meager rations of low-quality food, worked his fingers to the bone each day (except the Sabbath), and basically lived in a perpetual state of exhaustion.

Late one day, as Jeremiah was working in a field, he dropped to his knees in exhaustion while Jehoiachin walked by. Rather than jumping right back up and continuing to work, he had slumped down onto his knees breathing heavily, eyes closed, with sweat dripping from his face. From his left side he heard Jehoiachin shout, "Hey, slave, up and work!"

Jeremiah opened his eyes and just looked with an expression of shock, thinking to himself, "Hey, slave? Doesn't he know my name? We've been neighbors for years." His stupefied shock must have shown, because Jehoiachin swiftly adjusted his grip on his walking stick and approached.

"Up, slave, and work!"

"Jehoiachin, I'm your neighbor. Can't you use my name?"

A loud THWACK sounded out and Jeremiah's vision darkened. After a moment he realized he had been struck by Jehoiachin's walking stick. Again, shock pulsed through his mind in rhythm to the pulsing ache on the back of his head.

"Don't talk back to me. Up and work!"

Jeremiah was too stunned for words, and his shock

must still have shown because Jehoiachin lost all patience and began beating him furiously with the rod. The blows came again and again and again with vicious intensity. Pain began erupting out all over his body as the blows continued to rain down.

Eventually, darkness took Jeremiah and he knew nothing else.

When he awoke, he found himself lying on a rack in the slave quarters. He was being tended to by another slave, a woman, who had dressed his wounds. Slowly, his conscious mind began rising through the thick fog he found his thoughts wading through, but the fog was being replaced by the fires of searing pain. Pain from blows to his head. Pain from blows to his back. Pain from his arms, legs, chest, stomach ... it appeared that Jehoiachin had beaten every square inch of his body with that rod.

As his thoughts continued to clear, he found himself asking a question of the woman tending him even though he knew the answer. "What happened?"

"Jehoiachin beat you yesterday for your disobedience. You've been asleep for a little more than a day. That rod he carries is not for herding animals. It is for herding slaves."

"What is your name?"

"My name is Ruth."

"Ruth ... thank you for tending my wounds."

She rose and turned to leave. Jeremiah watched her go, and thought she was quite lovely and caring. A few moments later, Jehoiachin walked in and towered over his rack, rod in hand.

"Slave, did you learn something yesterday?"

"Yes, sir, I did. I'll not talk back or show any laziness ever again."

"Good, slave. Do not disappoint me. You've proved faithless in regard to the repayment of your loan. Do not prove faithless in your servitude to me." With that, he turned and stormed out.

Over the next couple of days, Jeremiah slowly improved. On the second day he was able to sit up and move more, and while the lacerations and bruising reached the peak of their ugliness, they had passed the peak of their pain. On the third day he was able to walk a bit. It was on the fifth day that he was able to move about somewhat normally again. Ruth must have been reporting regularly on his condition, because the morning of the sixth day, Jehoiachin entered at first light and sent him back to work.

The weeks and months since the beating passed, and Jeremiah continued living in his state of perpetual exhaustion. He had suffered no permanent physical injury from the beating, but his mind never forgot it. Ruth had been about now and then, and he had discovered that she was quite a faithful worker. Jehoiachin showed her special favor and placed his hands upon her in ways that most men would never dare to in Israel. Jeremiah's interest in her was turning romantic, despite his observations of this behavior.

During the third of his six years of servitude, Jeremiah approached Jehoiachin with a question.

"Sir, may I ask a question?"

"Yes, slave, you may. What is your question?"

"Ruth, may I have her for my wife? I believe that my service to you will be strengthened if I had a wife."

"I will consider your request. Do not ask me about it again. If I decide to give her to you, then you will know it. Otherwise, do not speak of or think about this again."

"Yes, sir, and thank you."

Months passed since Jeremiah had made his request. One day simply overflowed into the next as his bone-breaking work continued. Then, one Saturday evening after the sun had set and Sabbath ended, Jehoiachin approached him with Ruth in tow.

"Slave, you are immediately to move to the married slave quarters and take this woman to be your wife. Woman, go to your husband and continue to serve me well as his wife."

Although he sensed some bitterness in the giving, it was done. That was it. No ceremony. No gathering of family. No nothing. Another slave, who Jeremiah did not know, came and took him and Ruth to their tiny marriage quarters. They went in, consummated the marriage (although he recognized that the token of her virginity was not to be), and the next day both rose and went back to their arduous labors. Jeremiah took comfort in the fact that he would now have someone to share his life and labors with, and looked forward to the end of his servitude when he would return to his farm. He would not, he thought, now return alone. Now he would bring a wife ... and if they were lucky, children, too.

The years passed slowly, and Jeremiah and Ruth had two children, a daughter and a son. Working through the sixth year of his servitude, he counted the days as time ticked down to the completion of the agreed-upon period of slavery. At sundown on the Sabbath day that finally marked the return of his freedom, he stepped proudly out of the married slave quarters he occupied with Ruth and their children. Walking confidently, he went straight out to find Jehoiachin near the goat pasture. Seeing Jeremiah approach, the master spoke first.

"Jeremiah, the time of your service to me has ended. You may return to your farm to start your life fresh again."

"Thank you, Jehoiachin. I will depart immediately with my wife and children."

At that, Jehoiachin's expression hardened, and he shouted, *"NO! Your wife and children are my property. You will NOT take them. They must stay here."*

For the second time in six years, Jeremiah found himself too shocked to even move. Mouth agape, he simply stood there for several moments. Finally, finding his voice again, he said, *"Excuse me? My wife and children are your property?"*

"Yes, that is the law of Moses passed down for generations. If you come into slavery with a wife and children, then you may leave with your wife and children since they were your property before. My slaves are my property. Since I gave a slave to you for wife, both she and the children she bore remain my property and you can't take them. You can either work your farm for the years required to eventually earn enough money to buy them from me, or you can become my slave for life and stay here with them. A woman who has borne children will come at a very high price since she may yet bear more servants if I give her to someone else for a wife or have her for myself. You have until the next sundown to make your choice."

Jeremiah went to the community temple at first light the next morning to speak to the priest, who confirmed every word that Jehoiachin had spoken. According to the law of Moses, Ruth and the children did not belong to Jeremiah ... but to Jehoiachin. If Jeremiah decided to return to his farm and try to earn the money to buy them, then they might be given to another slave before he had earned *the money ... or Jehoiachin might take them for himself. Given his previous observations of Jehoiachin's behavior towards Ruth, he considered the latter possibility to be very likely. The only way he could be guaranteed to keep his wife and children was to go back into slavery ... for the rest of his life ... and the clock was ticking.*

Really, there was no decision open to him. What possible choice did he have? He loved Ruth. He loved his children. The thought of them being given to another man, or taken by Jehoiachin himself, was more than he could bear. He returned posthaste to Jehoiachin and committed himself to lifelong slavery. Jehoiachin performed the required ritual and bored through his ear with an awl while his head was against the doorpost and the judges of the community watched.

His farm became Jehoiachin's that day as well.

Thus, the poor honest farmer lost his property and freedom, but kept his wife and children. Thus, the dishonest and greedy man of wealth increased his property holdings and strengthened his grip on the small community.

At this point, the reader is probably aghast unless very familiar with the Bible. The reader may be thinking, "Wait, this is in the Bible? This kind of horrific crap is in the law that was supposedly passed down by a perfect and righteous god? You've got to be kidding me!" No, I'm not kidding. The horror of the story you just read is a simple illustration of what the god of the Bible commands in his law. For example, please open your Bible (or Bibles if you want to reference more than one version) and read Exodus 21:1–11, 20–21, 26–27, 32. These verses make quite clear the following points from the story I told above:

- Six years of service with the slave going free in the seventh, v. 2
- If a wife is given by the master, she and any children she bears remain the property of the master, v. 4
- A male slave can only keep a wife and children given by the master by "redeeming" them or by becoming the permanent lifelong slave of the master, vv. 5-6
- So long as no permanent injury is inflicted, a slave owner can beat his slaves with a rod so badly that it requires days of recovery (indeed, the slave can die after days of suffering) with zero punishment, vv. 20-21
- Female slaves do not have the right to go free in the seventh year, but will serve until death unless "redeemed" or given away in marriage, vv. 7-11

One typical argument presented by apologists is that this (and others like it, see Leviticus 25) is an obscure passage of the Old Testament, and therefore shouldn't be taken so seriously. This apologetic is nonsense. First, the context of the passage. Just turn one chapter back to Exodus 20 and you have the first introduction in scripture to what is now commonly known as the Ten Commandments. Consider that fact for just a moment ... the authors of the book of Exodus considered slavery to be so important that it literally follows right on the heels of the Ten Commandments. This is not, therefore, an obscure passage but is immediately in the context of commands considered to be so sacred that people try to erect them on government property in today's modern societies.

Another argument put forth by apologists is something along the lines of, "Well, this is the Old Testament and since Jesus fulfilled the law we shouldn't be too bothered by this. That was the old covenant, and now we have a new covenant." Once again, I say that is nonsense. Jesus had this to say about the law of the Old Testament in Matthew 5:17-19 (New American Standard Bible):

> Do not think that I came to abolish the Law or the Prophets; I did not come to abolish but to fulfill. For truly I say to you, until heaven and earth pass away, not the smallest letter or stroke shall pass from the Law until all is accomplished. Whoever then annuls one of the least of these commandments, and teaches others to do the same, shall be called least in the kingdom of heaven; but whoever keeps and teaches them, he shall be called great in the kingdom of heaven.

While it does say that he came to fulfill the law, it immediately explains that "not the smallest letter or stroke shall pass" and "whoever then annuls one of the least ... shall be called least." How then can the argument be made that an obscure passage doesn't matter? Jesus was quite clear above that anyone who advocates that the least command should be annulled would face consequences. In general, this is one of the myths about Jesus that Christians put forward on a regular basis. The myth that all of the horrific content in the Old Testament is somehow null and void due to the life and actions of Jesus. In his own words, however, he said exactly the opposite and warned people sternly against writing off any passages from the old covenant. This is one concept that groups like the cult I was in get right. If you write off one part of the Bible, then what is stopping anyone from writing off *any* part of the Bible?

One final apologetic argument to dismiss before moving on. Apologists further the second argument above by adding that the New Testament is a new covenant that supersedes the old. If the statement above from Jesus isn't enough to show that the old commands can't be annulled, then let's look at some other commands in the New Testament with regard to slavery.

Colossians 3:22-25 (New American Standard Bible)

Slaves, in all things obey those who are your masters on earth, not with external service, as those who merely please men, but with sincerity of heart, fearing the Lord. Whatever you do, do your work heartily, as for the Lord rather than for men, knowing that from the Lord you will receive the reward of the inheritance. It is the Lord Christ whom you serve. For he who does wrong will receive the consequences of the wrong which he has done, and that without partiality.

In the wonderful new covenant, you know the one they say absolved and annulled all of the horrific crap in the old one, slaves are commanded to obey their earthly masters. Note, the command is not, "Masters, what on earth are you thinking owning other human beings as slaves? Set them all free at once!" No, not that. The command is for the slave to obey. The new covenant does not abolish slavery. It affirms slavery and requires slaves to serve faithfully, even saying there will be divine punishment for failure to serve: "For he who does wrong will receive the consequences of the wrong which he has done, and that without partiality." No, the New Testament does not make this better. It serves to reinforce the narrative that slaves must obey masters and it does nothing whatsoever to start any kind of abolishment movement.

There are many other passages about slavery in the Bible, and as I progressed through the transition I've discussed in prior chapters, it was topics like this in the Bible that caused me to seriously question my faith. How could I believe that this god was some moral authority when his command permits one human being to own another as a form of property to the point that severe beatings go unpunished? This is a righteous god??? My initial decision, as previously discussed, was to decide that not everything in the Bible was from god. There were some good things, but clearly this couldn't be from god. The layers of the onion continued peeling back.

Genocide in the Bible

Magog was five. Five years old!!! He awoke in the morning excited and ran straight out to find his father roasting some eggs and meat over a fire. Leeks and onions sizzled on a piece of iron. Birthday breakfast! His mother was sitting nearby smiling at him while his little sister suckled at her breast. Her pregnancy belly made the perfect spot to rest his sister on while she drank.

"Happy birthday!" said his father excitedly. "What do you want to do to—"

His father's words were cut off by the sound of a horn blaring. It was the community guard sounding an alarm for a raid. The pattern being blown on the horn could mean only one thing ... the Israelites were coming!!! Shouts began rising throughout their city, and Magog could hear swords, shields, and armor being readied in the clamor. His mother held him by the hand and carried his sister as they ran into their home to hide.

Shouting that he loved them, his father donned his helmet and armor, grabbed his spear, and ran off towards the city walls. The horns of Israel could now be heard in the distance and the shouting of a large army was growing louder. Men were running past their home in growing numbers as they mustered the defense of the city.

Magog was terrified. Tears streamed down his cheeks as he huddled in a corner with his mother. The horrible noise outside was growing louder and louder. Metal clashing and screeching against metal and countless men not only shouting but screaming in agony. The fighting went on for hours, and although they had all stopped crying, he was still huddled in the corner with his pregnant mother and baby sister while she slowly rocked back and forth with them.

Fighting continued through the entire day, and the sound was getting louder and louder, closer and closer while the sun dipped towards the horizon. The sounds of fighting seemed to be coming from the streets just outside their house, but it wasn't just the screams of men he heard. He also heard women and children screaming in horror.

Magog started crying again. This was his birthday!!! Why did this have to happen? Where was his father?

Suddenly, as the sounds of fighting seemed to rise just outside their very house, the door burst open and his father staggered backwards into their home while he, his sister, and his mother all screamed in terror. His father was bleeding heavily from his left side just under his armpit. He thrust his spear forward with his right, stabbing an Israelite through the throat, but two more sprang in and killed his father with their swords. Magog simply could not stop screaming. His pregnant mother rose and stepped in front of him and his sister, while the Israelite soldiers glared.

His mother began screaming, "Not my children! SPARE MY CHILDREN!!!" One of the soldiers stepped forward, and swung with his sword, cleaving his mother's throat through and sending a fountain of blood onto his sister. The other soldier had stepped forward and grabbed his sister, plunging his sword into her stomach. They then both looked at Magog standing there screaming with tears streaming down his face. Fire erupted in Magog's belly as the first soldier thrust his sword point forward. Blood-filled vomit erupted from the boy's mouth as the fire in his gut intensified and his vision fogged over. The last thing little Magog perceived as darkness took him was his mother's body on the floor in front of him, blood pooled around her head and vacant eyes staring at nothing in particular. He gave one final tiny whimper, and then passed into darkness.

The Israelites slaughtered every last person in Magog's village that night. Men, women, children ... even babies like his sister. They also slaughtered every single animal, and then put fire to the city when they were ready to move on. But Jehovah, their god, was not pleased. Was it the murder and mayhem that displeased this perfect and righteous being? No. Was it the merciless slaughter of every single infant and child? No. The following displeased their god: the Israelites let the king of the enemy survive, and they allowed the best of the animals to survive. This is what displeased their god. Instead of completing the genocide, they left one surviving human, and the finest of the animals survived as well. This infinitesimal mercy did not please Jehovah. Complete and utter genocide is what he wanted.

There are passages in the Bible where genocide is documented. These passages recording a history are merely a recounting of events as they took place. These historical passages don't pose a moral conundrum for Christianity because they do not speak either in favor of or against the deeds done. They are intended merely to recount what is supposed to be a matter of fact, much like a geologist's description of Pompei being destroyed by Vesuvius. A record of events is simply that and makes no moral judgments. Nature ... facts ... are amoral. They make no qualitative judgments. They simply are.

However, there are deeply disturbing passages in scripture where not only is a genocidal act recorded but is directly commanded by the god of the Bible. This is very different and absolutely *does* pose a profound moral dilemma for Christianity. The story told above, which should have left the reader deeply disturbed, is a direct illustration of one such passage where not only is a genocide recorded, but that genocide is directly commanded by Jehovah, the god of Israel. Not only is that genocide commanded by the god of Israel, but he is also displeased because it was not carried out to the letter by King Saul. 1 Samuel 15:1-3 (New American Standard Bible) has the following command of Jehovah:

> Then Samuel said to Saul, "The LORD sent me to anoint you as king over His people, over Israel; now therefore, listen to the words of the Lord." Thus says the LORD of hosts, "I will punish Amalek for what he did to Israel, how he set himself against him on the way while he was coming up from Egypt. Now go and strike Amalek and utterly destroy all that he has, and do not spare him; but put to death both man and woman, child and infant, ox and sheep, camel and donkey."

Consider those words from the deity who, if we are to believe the evangelicals, is ardently pro-life. Essentially, god himself commands that every single human being be slaughtered mercilessly in an act of genocide ... and this deity specifically names infants. What can possibly be said in defense of such a horrific command? We are told today that god is love. God is mercy. God is righteous. Really? This god??? The one who commanded a genocide so horrific one would think we were reading an edict written by Pol Pot, Adolf Hitler, Josef Stalin, or Idi Amin? Slaughter the entire city without even sparing the children and infants ... even kill all the animals, too???

Once again, a passage in the Bible caused me to seriously question what I believed. The god I worshipped commanded this? How could I possibly reconcile this? Reading the Bible for what it says can indeed drive someone toward atheism, and I was being driven in that direction by an increasing perception that Jehovah was an immoral thug, not a perfectly righteous being of love and mercy.

Sex Slavery in the Bible

Exhaustion overwhelmed Delilah's senses. The day before, she, her younger sister, and their three brothers had ridden with their father on horses through their pastureland. Since they raised sheep, it was important to go and make sure the flocks were being well tended by the shepherds they hired. At age eight, this was her younger sister's first time riding out (she sat in front of her father on his horse). Her older brother (ten) rode with their eldest brother (eighteen). Delilah (twelve) and her other brother (fifteen) had ridden alone. It was her first time solo on a horse and she was very excited. Her mother, of course, having borne five children and being pregnant with a sixth, was in no condition to ride out with them. She stayed at their home tending to matters there.

The riding was rough at times over uneven ground as they passed up and down over the hills, but Delilah still had a wonderful day. Upon returning home near the end of the day, she, her mother, and her sister were washing up and began discussing matters of feminine hygiene. A small issue of blood had come from her younger sister's most sacred area. It was too early for the time of her adulthood to arrive, so her mother became concerned. Her mother told her sister, "You were injured while riding the horses. This is not your monthly flow. It will heal. We will have to explain this one day when you are given in marriage so your future husband will understand that you are a virgin, even though the token of your virginity is now gone." Delilah did not understand this completely but had some idea of what her mother meant. She put it out of her mind. Around their home and land, the other Midianites were quieting down for the night.

Little did she know how horrific the consequences of this injury would be the next day.

Early the next morning, the family was awakened by shouting as the sun came up. The Israelites were attacking. Quickly, their small, scattered community tried to make some defense against the invading army. As the light continued to brighten, however, they could see smoke rising from the direction of other nearby Midianite camps ... other clans they knew that had already been attacked during the night.

There was really no battle at all in their community. Delilah, her mother, and her sister huddled in their small tent while they heard men shouting. Her father and brothers had ridden out, with the exception of her ten-year-old youngest brother, but had not returned. Shortly after the fighting had started, it was clear that Israel had easily won the battle with their small community. All of the men had been slain. Israel was gathering up all of the survivors, as well as the flocks and herds, and many of the prized possessions of the Midianites from many communities and preparing to take it all as plunder back to their own people.

Upon being brought to the massive Israelite camp east of Jordan in the land of Moab, the livestock and valuables were taken away while survivors were organized into *groups. Moses was coming, along with the high priests. He looked furious and was shouting in Hebrew. Delilah was too far away to make out what was being said, but it didn't sound pleasant. Without warning, the sound of many swords being drawn erupted around them, and Israelite soldiers began moving through the groups of captive Midianites.*

They were slaughtering all the little boys (including babies), and all of the older women. Screams of terror and agony mixed incoherently with cries for mercy as the bloodbath continued. Every woman who was obviously a mother was cut down without mercy, even if they were pregnant. Younger women, however, whose virginity was questionable were inspected first. While their family members and neighbors lay dead or dying around them, an Israelite soldier would inspect the younger woman's most private and sacred of areas. If the inspection was completed and the tokens of her virginity were not present, she was cut down where she stood without hesitation. If those tokens were present, then she would be separated out with the other terrified and sobbing girls. When the soldiers reached her family, her ten-year-old brother grabbed a stick from the ground and swung it at the approaching soldier. This rather young-looking soldier easily parried the stick with his sword, and then struck, hewing her brother's head from the top of his neck in a fountain of blood. Next, he turned on her pregnant mother and stabbed his sword through her chest, killing both her and her unborn child in the process.

When the young man turned towards Delilah, other men grabbed her by both arms and held her. The young man bent and began performing his inspection of her most sacred area. The sense of violation ... of invasion ... was so perverse in her that she vomited. After finding the tokens of her virginity intact, he moved on to her eight-year-old sister. With horror dawning in her mind, she remembered the words her mother had spoken the day before. The tokens of her little sister's virginity would not be found because of the horseback riding injury.

Delilah began screaming in horror, "She was injured riding a horse! It's an injury!!! AN INJURY!!!!!"

Her screams were of no avail. After the inspection, the young soldier stabbed her little sister through the abdomen with his sword, leaving her screaming and dying on the ground. They moved off through the group of terrified survivors performing their horrific inspect-kill-inspect-capture-inspect-kill pattern.

Delilah was dragged to the location where the other bloodied, violated, and weeping young women were all being held. Later, when the genocide was complete, the soldiers all returned. The captives, as well as all the soldiers who had done the killing, were kept separate from the main Israelite camp for seven days. The young Midianite girls were given food, water, and supplies so they could stay clean and care for themselves during this time, but they were also kept under guard to prevent them from escaping.

At the end of the seven days, the elders, along with the soldiers, approached the survivors of the genocidal battle. The elders began working through the surviving girls, pointing at them and sending them away with soldiers. What was happening? When it came to her, an elder pointed at her and a young man approached. Delilah realized with growing horror that this was the same man who had murdered her entire family right in front of her and violated her body. The young man took her and turned away, walking with her as she wept in a mixture of shock, terror, and grief. They walked through the camp, eventually approaching a small tent. The young man turned and spoke to her. "I am Elihu, and you are my wife. Come in unto me."

"Wait, what?! WIFE???" Her mind screamed, but there was nothing she could do. He dragged her inside as she screamed and wept. The murderer of her pregnant mother, sister, and youngest brother inexorably forced her into his tent ... and then mercilessly raped her.

This was now her life. She was the bride of the very man who had murdered the people dearest to her right before her eyes. She would bear his children. She would never escape.

Within one year of these events, Delilah would take her own life in order to end her daily torment.

At this point, the reader is probably even more disturbed than after reading the last two narratives. The slaughter commanded by the god of the Bible is bad enough in a passage like 1 Samuel 15 but adding the forced marriage of young girls to the very people that murdered their families is an altogether worse detail to add. Yet, that is exactly what happened in Numbers 31. God, through the prophet Moses, directly commands the slaughter of all of the Midianites (keep in mind, Moses's own wife was a Midianite according to scripture). The passage is too long to cite in its entirety here, but below are some of the key verses to consider when evaluating the kind of moral character attributed to Jehovah in the Bible. All verses below come from Numbers 31 in the New American Standard Bible:

- "Then the LORD spoke to Moses, saying, 'Take full vengeance for the sons of Israel on the Midianites; afterward you will be gathered to your people.' " vv. 1–2
- "The sons of Israel captured the women of Midian and their little ones; and all their cattle and all their flocks and all their goods they plundered. Then they burned all their cities where they lived and all their camps with fire. They took all the spoil and all the prey, both of man and of beast." vv. 9–11
- "Moses and Eleazar the priest and all the leaders of the congregation went out to meet them outside the camp. Moses was angry with the officers of the army, the captains of thousands and the captains of hundreds, who had come from service in the war. And Moses said to them, 'Have you spared all the women? Behold, these caused the sons of Israel, through the counsel of Balaam, to trespass against the LORD in the matter of Peor, so the plague was among the congregation of the LORD. Now therefore, kill every male among the little ones, and kill every woman who has known man intimately. But all the girls who have not known man intimately, spare for yourselves.' " vv. 13–18

There you have it. God commands Moses to commit this genocidal act. Afterwards, Moses is *not* angry that they slaughtered every adult male mercilessly with no prisoners. No, that is not the cause of his anger. He is angered because he wanted the army to go *further* in their genocide. To be clear, he is not angry because they committed a merciless act that would be considered a war crime by today's standards. He is angry because he wanted them to commit an even deeper atrocity and they did not. This is why he gives them a further command. Of the captives that they have with them, they are to kill every last male no matter how young. Of the female captives, they are to slaughter all but the virgins. The virgins, they can forcibly marry and rape to their heart's content.

It was during my time of suffering through infertility, and other challenges, that I began questioning these horrors in the book I still considered sacred. Why did I consider it so holy when it contained such *unholy* garbage? Why was I still holding on to this thing after all these years? At the end of the day, I simply stopped making excuses for these moral horrors, took them at face value, and realized that if a god did write this book, it was not a god I wanted anything to do with.

Can people be led to atheism by honestly reading the Bible for themselves? Yes, it absolutely can happen. However, most ardent fundamentalists already *have* read the book and just make excuses for the horrors they read. I was one such person for many years. Because of my own history, therefore, of having read it and made excuses of various kinds for over a decade, I don't think this is the best way to proceed for someone who is of a more fundamentalist bent. Rather, as I said earlier in the chapter, I believe a concurrent study of Bible translation and canonization will be more effective for such a person.

How is the Bible Translated?

In the Assembly, but very late in my tenure there, I had begun reading about the history of how various translations came to be. However, that reading had not involved much detail. For example, it was years after the Assembly that I had read about the fact that Martin Luther had adamantly insisted that the book of James should not be included in canon because of its emphasis on "faith without works is dead." The first book I read on the subject was about the King James Version and how it came to be. I was fascinated, in particular, by the political conflict surrounding the project. While the translators were left free by the throne to make sure it was accurate overall, there were certain sections edited and massaged specifically to emphasize the power of kings on a throne, their appointment by god to the seat of that power, etc.

There is a myth among evangelical fundamentalists, a myth I myself once believed, about how Bible translation works. The myth goes that the original documents written by the original authors are kept in vaults somewhere, and that these documents (including the original gospel manuscripts that they believe are actually written by Matthew, Mark, Luke, and John, for example) are used by modern translators to facilitate the painstaking work of creating new translations of scripture in modern languages.

I call this a myth because it is patently false.

The first fact to dispel this myth (which anyone can easily research and confirm for themselves) is this: we have quite literally *zero* of the original documents for any book, passage, or single verse of the Bible. *All* of the original parchments, scraps of document, etc. have been lost to the depths of time. When translators do their work, therefore, they are simply *not* using the original works as written by the original authors.

In addition, the second fact to dispel this myth is the overwhelming majority of modern scholars believe that the traditionally *accepted* authors of the books of the Bible were not in fact the *actual* authors of these stories. Matthew did not write Matthew. Moses did not write the first five books of the Bible (Genesis, Exodus, Leviticus, Numbers, and Deuteronomy). Daniel did not write Daniel. If you do the scholarly research, you find that it is firmly believed we do not know who actually wrote these books.

When a new translation is created, what actually takes place is that a given body of translators working together as a team have a number of different ancient manuscripts to work from. These manuscripts are often missing significant sections. Not only are they missing sections, but they also (and this is very important to understand clearly) DO NOT AGREE WITH EACH OTHER!!! A translator must, therefore, use multiple manuscripts such that where a section of a passage is missing in one, it can be filled in from another that does not have that section missing. In addition, where manuscripts disagree with one another, the team of translators will decide how to word a passage in modern languages based on some compromise that is believed to be the clearest meaning derived by comparing the various competing sections of a given passage.

One clear example of this that is cited in the marginal notes of most translations is from the Gospel according to John (which was *not*, scholars believe, written by John). If you open whatever translation(s) you have in your home to John 7:53 – 8:11 there will be a marginal note on this passage. It is one of the most beloved and most regularly cited passages amongst American evangelicals. It is the story of the woman caught in the act of adultery in which Jesus utters the immortal phrase, "He among you who is without sin, let him cast the first stone." The Pharisees bring her before Jesus.

(Side note: where was the man? If she was caught in adultery, she had to be caught *with* someone, so where was the other person? Guess only women needed to be killed for adultery back then ... Anyway, back to the story ...)

This violent mob of people led by the religious leaders of Jerusalem brought her there with the express intention of stoning her to death on the spot. God's righteous judgment in action ... kill them dead ... and do it right now. Jesus famously says to them, "He who is without sin among you, let him be the first to throw a stone at her." They all walk away, and the woman goes free. This passage of mercy in the midst of a bloodthirsty society is profound for many reasons from a storytelling perspective. However, there is something else to note from the margins of most translations. In my New American Standard Bible, the margin of this passage has the following to say: "Later manuscripts add the story of the adulterous woman, numbering it as John 7:53 – 8:11." My American Standard Bible says this in the margins: "Most of the ancient authorities omit John 7:53 – 8:11. Those which contain it vary much from each other." Finally, the New International Version places clear brackets around this section of John in addition to including a comment about the oldest manuscripts not including the verses in question. In other words, when a team of translators is working through the documents used to create modern translations, the most ancient of texts available *do not have this story in them.* This story, therefore, *must* have been added later. Knowing this, there are actually a number of modern translations that leave this story out or bracket it to formally call out the fact that it very much appears the story is missing from the oldest manuscripts available and was likely not included in the original document.

There are a number of common phrases in society that come from this very story. "Casting stones" is one of them. How amazing is it, therefore, to learn that the story was almost certainly not part of the original document? Added later as an imaginative afterthought, this story has inspired uncounted numbers of sermons through the ages. This story is almost certainly just that ... a story. Without any doubt upon learning that it was added later, one must conclude that this event in all likelihood never took place and is just imaginative storytelling taken too literally.

One of the most often cited examples of this "the ancient documents are perfect and complete" myth, and one of the easiest to definitively disprove, is the Dead Sea Scrolls. American evangelical fundamentalists will often say something like the following (I used to say it back in the day): "The Dead Sea Scrolls prove that what we have in the Bible is accurate!!!" This is, once again, a patently false statement. It is a myth. First, the book of Esther is completely missing from the collection of ancient parchments. The fact that an *entire book* included in the modern Old Testament is just missing completely is *not* confirmation of 100 percent accuracy of modern Bibles. It is quite the opposite. In addition, there are as a matter of fact significant differences in many of the story/textual details between the Dead Sea Scrolls and other ancient manuscripts used for Bible translation. A simple source like Quora has a number of good articles on this subject, and even a simple review of formal scholarship on the subject shows the same.

Finally, the Dead Sea Scrolls are a perfect illustration of the discussion in the earlier paragraphs of missing portions from documents. On the prior page and above are a few images of the actual Dead Sea Scrolls. Anyone can find these and other images online via a very simple search, and then confirm their authenticity by reviewing scholarly works on the subject. As the reader can clearly see from these images, even the most intact of these parchments contain missing pieces that scholars must "best guess" translation from. If words are missing, a translator must make an educated guess from context and from other available ancient documents as to what the missing pieces say. These facts are a perfect illustration of translation of the Bible as a whole. Texts are incomplete. Texts disagree with one another. Scholars must compare, contrast, and best guess as to the most-clear rendering into modern languages from these ancient documents.

Modern Bible translations, therefore, are *not* created from perfect, infallible, universally agreed-upon ancient documents. The idea that they are is a very common myth spread among Christians, and it was something that I actively believed and spread at one time without doing any research at all to see if what I believed was actually true. Realizing this fact was a cornerstone change for me in my thinking about the Bible and how to interpret it. It actually happened in my first read-through of the updated NASB. For whatever reason, as I was reading the Gospel of John for the umpteenth time (it was my favorite book of the Bible), I actually checked the marginal note on chapter 7:53 – 8:11. The marginal note, cited a few pages back, rocked me. I was already to the point where I was a liberal Christian who no longer took the Bible literally, but the fact that the oldest documents simply did not have this story in them sent me into research mode. I was able to quickly confirm the first sentence of this paragraph (took a few hours one Saturday sometime in mid-2009).

Immediately, I was forced to face some pretty significant questions ... questions which served to reinforce my evolving idea that the Bible simply cannot be a literal account of events.

- If the original documents no longer even exist, what of the belief I held for years that the Bible in its original form is infallible? This was something we said to excuse mistakes and contradictions between translations. The translations may be fallible, but the *original* documents were inerrant. Didn't the fact that we don't even have the originals create a problem with this position?

- If the oldest documents we have now don't universally agree with each other, even in beloved and commonly cited stories like the woman caught in adultery, are there any biblical narratives that we can trust to be 100 percent accurate?
- If we can't trust the narratives to be 100 percent accurate, how historical an account is the Bible as a whole?
- Finally, given the likelihood of error inherent in both the ancient manuscripts and the translation process, why do I believe any of this any more than other ancient religious texts like the Quran or the Bhagavad Gita?

These and other questions circulated in my mind as I continued doing research into the scholarship of various Bible translations. Not only was I confronting the horrors of genocidal fury attributed to the god of the Bible, but I was also learning that the text was not the historically reliable document that I had once believed it to be ... and all the while my wife and I continued to suffer through miscarriage after miscarriage with no answer to our prayers.

Who Decided that These Books Belonged in the Bible?

This is a complicated question, and I will in no way do it justice here. Other, more scholarly minded people have done much more thorough and authoritative work on this subject. I mention it here solely because I am discussing the impact of various topics on my personal journey. Learning how people through the ages have decided what works belong in inspired scripture or don't helped push me away from faith.

There is a profound level of disagreement between the various flavors of Christianity (and related religions) with regard to what represents "inspired inerrant scripture" and what does not. Keep in mind that the disagreements between various sects of Christianity about what belongs in the Bible to begin with further muddy the aforementioned issues with translation even of what is accepted by any given group. Orthodox Christians of various shades accept books in their Old Testament that Catholics do not, while Catholics accept books that Protestants do not, and Protestants accept books that Samaritans do not, and so on. First, therefore, Christians don't even agree which books belong in scripture to begin with, much less how to translate those books. Why, then, should we accept the verdict of men (women were excluded from the positions of power in the church) about which books are actually divine when they could not even agree on that point amongst themselves? As mentioned previously, Martin Luther vigorously opposed the inclusion of the book of James because of its emphasis on works. He also wanted to remove Hebrews, Jude, and Revelation from scripture since he felt they stood in opposition to some standard Christian theology and doctrine. A good many others did not want Revelation included either because it is just so crazy and outlandish. If one takes the time to research why certain books were included while others were not, it doesn't take long to discover the level of church and secular politics involved, the level of personal opinions and bias, and the plain fact that these were just men making the decision ... no god necessary.

While my wife and I were suffering the hardships associated with our infertility journey, I was continuing my detailed study of the Bible and expanding that study beyond mere scripture to include the topics discussed in this chapter. Absolutely horrific atrocities are directly ascribed to the god of the Bible, and he is good? Translation of the books of the Bible is not the clear-cut process most evangelicals imagine, so can we really rely on the very book we have in our hands? Men, often motivated by matters of politics and power, are the ones who decided what should or should not be in scripture. Why should we accept their decisions on this subject? It was the combination of everything I was experiencing personally, as well as this other study that eventually led us to become atheists.

Both of us can honestly tell you today that we are far happier for the decision.

People often suffer a feeling of loss nearing the level of the death of a loved one when losing their faith. For us, we were so numb from our losses overall that while we felt something was missing, we also had a new sense of purpose. We began restructuring our lives and removing the trappings of religious tradition. These religious traditions, we then began replacing with new traditions that we created for ourselves based on who we were individually and as a couple. One thing we always did as Christians, for example, was pray before our meals. Replacing a religious tradition with something else was really important as it eliminated that feeling of something being missing. So, Chanthy and I sat down and created a family saying. We now recite this before our meals instead of praying (and it is so cute hearing our four-year-old son learning it at mealtime). There is psychological power in the recitation of words as a group. This is why all religious groups have some form or other of this tradition. Whether singing of communal songs, reciting liturgies or legends ... many voices joining together as one has power for human beings. Here is our family saying, which we say before every meal. I think this is a fitting way to end this chapter:

> We are family
> We find our joy in each other
> We find our hope in our future
> We find our peace in our lives together
> We love each other
> Now and always

Chapter Nine
A Joy Realized

During the months leading up to the donor IVF cycle (described in chapter seven) we had discussed extensively what to do if it failed. We only had the financial resources for one of two options, to say nothing of the emotional capacity to deal with yet another confirmed miscarriage. Either 1) we would attempt another, even more aggressive and expensive fertility cycle, or 2) we would adopt. Should we choose another fertility cycle, and should that cycle fail, we would not have the resources for another cycle or for adoption. The reality of my sperm DNA problem essentially made the decision for us, and as we recovered from our loss during the spring of 2016, we also simultaneously planned for our adoption process. This time we would end up parents. No question about it. No matter how long it took, we would adopt and finally have a precious child of our own. Also, as a side benefit, Chanthy's body would not suffer any of the negative side effects of pregnancy and childbirth.

Pregnancy and childbirth take a huge toll on a woman's body, and there are permanent changes that take place that any birth mother will live with for the rest of her life. With adoption, Chanthy would not suffer any of these side effects of pregnancy and childbirth, and we would end up parents at the end of the process. It was only a matter of time. This reality gave us a new hope and purpose amidst our realization that we were atheists. Combined with the new traditions we were slowly introducing into our lives, this new hope provided by our adoption project really drove us forward with intensely focused purpose.

First decision ... domestic adoption or international? We decided on domestic adoption mostly because international was so much more complicated and fraught with legal and logistical perils uncounted. In international adoption, the adoptive parents are typically presented with a list of potential children to adopt. The parents choose a child and then begin working towards bringing that child home. There are lots of unknowns in this process. In particular, if one is dealing with a corrupt government, one may be receiving falsified information about the potential child. One might be told that a child is a given young age. However, after bringing the child home, one might find that the child is as small as the given age because he or she is extremely malnourished and very small for their age. As a result, one can't always trust those international sources of information.

In domestic adoption, the birth parents are provided with a list of prospective adopters (the exact opposite of international). The birth parents decide who they feel is best suited to care for their child. As adoptive parents, it may be some time before a set of birth parents decide you are the best option. You enter into the quest not knowing how long it may take for a set of birth parents to choose you. However, at the end of the day you can be reasonably assured that (no matter how long it takes) you will almost certainly be chosen and a child will be yours. In case you are curious, domestic infant adoption takes the average couple six to twelve months from the time an agency approves you as prospective parents to the time there is a match with a child.

This was our hope. Finally, even if it took a few years, we *would* be parents. We worried about a whole host of things. In 2016 when we began the registration process for adoption, I was thirty-nine and my wife thirty-eight. We worried that our age might play a part as potential birth parents often choose younger people. Given our interethnic status, with me being white and my wife Cambodian, we also worried that race might play a part in any decisions made by birth parents. Finally, having just become atheists (but not out of the closet yet), another worry was that a young Christian who was giving up a child might reject us for religious reasons.

Wait, the reader might ask, young Christians are often giving up children for adoption? Yes, that is absolutely the case. The Bible Belt, and the more religious areas of our country as a whole, have far higher rates of unplanned pregnancy than the liberal areas. It's true ... the more evangelical the area, the more unplanned pregnancies there are. The state of Texas has some of the strongest abstinence-only education in the United States. It also has not only the highest rate of teen pregnancy in the nation (per capita) but the highest rate of *repeat* teen pregnancy. Where conservative Christian movements have a larger presence and more political influence, social issues like unplanned pregnancy and abortion are *more* common (per capita), not less. This goes completely against their narrative that the moral teachings they hold make society better, but that could be a book in and of itself.

Having said that about our worries, however, we had some very strong factors in our favor. One, I have a very successful career. As a senior executive for a successful publicly traded company, our financial resources are quite strong. We were, at the time, heavily leveraged due to our infertility debt, but we were confident in our ability to work out of it. This would give any birth parents no concerns whatsoever that their child might somehow be impoverished or otherwise not provided for properly. Chanthy had a very successful career before we married, and she decided to be a homemaker. As the reader may recall, she and I met at a medical device company in Silicon Valley. She was the executive admin for the research and development team, which had over thirty engineers. As her manager quite seriously said, she was the reason that department ran so smoothly. It was her work, her detail-oriented mind, her intelligent thoroughness, and her dedication that kept them all working. Since both she and I were successful businesspeople, this would play heavily in our favor. We were married in order to try to start a family, so she made the decision to become a homemaker rather than keep working.

She still gets job offers today, some very tempting, but turns them down.

Another advantage is the area where we live. Just outside of Sacramento, when the roads are clear, we can be at North Lake Tahoe in ninety minutes or South Lake Tahoe in two hours. We can also make the drive to San Francisco in about two and a half hours. Essentially, we can go anywhere from city to beach to snow to mountain hiking to desert and even to Disneyland in an easy day's drive from the quiet community where we live. We believed that adoptive parents would find our situation desirable for their child, despite the concerns noted earlier.

Most domestic adoption agencies give adoptive parents various options for their process. This is partly to tailor the adoption to cultural, religious, or other social requirements of the prospective parents. It is also intended to provide support for various budgetary restrictions. Each more selective decision made by parents-to-be has the potential to do two things. First, the process will likely take longer. Second, the process will likely be more expensive. For example, if parents choose the sex of the child they want, they are automatically eliminating roughly 50 percent of potential children from the adoption pool. This, we were told, serves to double the estimated time it will take to adopt, and most agencies will charge an additional fee. As a result, we only made health-based selections with regard to our potential child.

No restrictions based on sex.

No restrictions based on ethnicity.

No restrictions based on where in the country the child would come from.

No restrictions based on the religion of the birth parents.

Our only restrictions revolved around the health of the birth parents. Since alcoholism, illicit drugs, and smoking have very serious potential complications for the health of a child born, we selected against being matched with birth parents who have abuse of these things in their history. This, we were told, would likely extend our process. You see, a large number of unplanned pregnancies come from people living these lifestyles. As a result, our choices might delay the process. However, we felt very strongly that waiting even months longer was more important than adopting a child with developmental challenges associated with the substance abuse of the birth parents.

The process began with evaluations for us. Were we healthy? Were we financially stable? Were we emotionally and psychologically stable both individually and as a whole in our marital relationship? We were evaluated by professionals for all of these things, and they evaluated our home to make sure it was safe for a child to live in. After passing these quite thorough evaluations we moved on to the next step.

Preparing ourselves to be marketed to birth parents was next. We received a video camera from a production company and were instructed to record ourselves engaging in various activities in the area where we lived. We took our mountain bikes to the local creek and recorded ourselves riding with egrets, herons, and ducks swimming in the background. We asked some friends to record us playing board games with their son, and hiking through the coastal redwoods up in Humboldt County. Our families recorded themselves making statements of love and support. It was really stressful, but we were extremely excited to be going forward. We started the evaluation process in May of 2016, and by August of that year we were approved and our personal marketing web page, complete with narratives, photos, and videos, was up on the agency website and active. We were told that between February and August of 2017, we would be parents if the law of averages held sway.

Something else happened late in 2016. We had been

house hunting for some time, and we finally found a great starter home. It was 2,056 square feet, had a pool, and the kitchen was nicely remodeled. We jumped on it. In November 2016 Chanthy and I moved into the first home we purchased together. Spending money on some new furniture, we got it nicely appointed ... and then had it re-evaluated by the adoption agency since they once again had to opine on whether or not our new home was safe. That year, we spent the Christmas season completing our move-in process and preparing our home for our child-to-be. It was exciting.

Shortly after the new year, as an accountant, I am at my busiest time of year. With the projects of both going through the annual audit and preparing our annual Form 10K for the Securities and Exchange Commission, I do not take time off during January or February of any year. It is simply too busy.

Then, on Friday, January 13th, 2017, the phone rang (yes, Friday the 13th). It was the adoption agency. A young couple from Kansas had selected us. We needed to drop everything and buy a plane ticket for January 17th so we could fly to Kansas City and be present for the birth of our son. Joy and terror flooded my mind. Now? Right now??? I'm so busy! What am I going to do??? I called the CEO of the company and told him the news. He very graciously, and very joyfully, told me to take the time necessary, and that we would delay our filing to the last deadline so Chanthy and I could go meet our son. We would be in Kansas for anywhere from ten to fourteen days, depending on how long the legal process took.

WE WERE GOING TO BE PARENTS IN JUST A FEW DAYS!!!!!

Already, we had invested in a large number of nonperishable supplies for the time when we would bring home a child. My wife immediately began unpacking and preparing these and other items in the room we had set up for a baby. The day before we left, we hit the store and bought some perishable items to put in the fridge that we hoped would still be unspoiled by the time we returned. With a potential two-week turnaround time, we weren't holding our breath.

As the Southwest Airlines flight lifted off from Sacramento International Airport, we began to quietly cry while holding hands. Passing over the Sierra Nevada and then out east over the Great Basin, the Rockies, and finally the Great Plains, the ground below was mantled in white snow for much of the flight. There was no snow in Kansas when we arrived, but it was quite cold compared to what we were used to. We drove through territory foreign to us, buying flowers at a floral shop owned and operated by a man who, it turned out, was himself adopted.

Upon arriving at the hospital, our hearts were hammering in our chests. Up the elevator we went, and into the room we walked where the birth parents were seated, talking. Warm and heartfelt introductions were made. We talked, told them about the name we had chosen and what it meant to us, and as it turned out we had arrived mere minutes before the main event. The nurse excused us from the room and we went to wait. For what seemed like an eternity, we sat with the aunt of the birth father (the young couple, ages twenty and twenty-one, were not married). They already had one son together and simply could not afford a second child. Keeping their second son would result in taking food out of the mouth of the first that they were already struggling to support. That's why they had made the decision to give him up for adoption, and that decision made us parents.

After what seemed like an eternity, we were welcomed back into the room where both Chanthy and I cried and smiled while holding our son in our arms. Chanthy went with the nurse and took video while our son received his first bath. I stood outside the glass smiling and talking with the birth father. That night, the hospital was not busy, so we were allowed to stay in a room with our new son. We spent a largely sleepless night with our newborn son, lying on uncomfortable beds, and practically freaking out at every odd sound coming from his bed.

The next morning, the birth parents left to return to their home and we remained with our son. I had set up a very odd little workstation for myself so that I could keep doing some work on my current company's Form 10K and audit. It was exhausting. Worrying about work. Worrying about our newborn. Worrying about my exhausted wife who was losing much more sleep than I. Since I was the driver while we were there, it was important for me to try to get some sleep at least. The hospital kept us around again the night of January 18th, but the next morning we were allowed to leave.

Wait, we're leaving the hospital ... alone and unsupervised by nursing staff ... WITH A BABY???

The State of Kansas had not yet given us the green light to return home to California. We were told by the agency to make ourselves comfortable at a nice hotel. We would be around for at least another week, possibly two. Near the Kansas City Speedway, there were some nicer hotels. We stayed at a Hampton Inn there. Describing that week is very difficult. We were both sleep-deprived, and I was crazy busy trying to manage the audit process and financial filing. The days blurred together and our memories of the time are just not entirely clear. My dear wife worked so hard to make that week happy, as did I. However, settling into a hotel (rather than our comfortable home with our two dogs) in a completely unfamiliar city and state, where white people were obviously giving my wife shit just for having brown skin ... in a great many respects, despite the joy of finally being parents, it was not a fun time.

Those days at the hotel passed very slowly. We were together, and we were getting to know our son. Anyone who has cared for a newborn will understand when I say that something of his personality was already emerging. He slept almost constantly, but when his eyes were open, he just stared as newborns do. We had two queen beds in our room, and there was a desk where I set up my portable printer and laptop. I was working and helping my wife out. I was running out for food since the hotel food left much to be desired. There were a couple of decent restaurants nearby, but it was the off-season. Zero racing takes place at the speedway in January, so most of the nearby businesses were either closed or open with limited hours. The roads were a disaster. Disrepair was everywhere from the highways to the back roads. Getting around often meant driving where the navigation system was leading, only to find a road blocked by "construction in progress" signs, leaving me with no choice but to find a way around and try again. Since virtually everything was closed down, we went to the same three or four restaurants for the entire duration of our stay. Fortunately, the restaurant right outside the hotel was both good (Famous Dave's BBQ) and open all the time since there was a lively night scene there. It was one of perhaps two restaurants that we found while we were there that had consistent hours. We probably sampled that BBQ restaurant's entire menu during our stay.

We have this to say about the hotel staff of Hampton Inn, Kansas City ... they knew we were there to adopt our baby boy, and they treated us with the utmost professionalism and kindness. We have nothing but praise for everything they did for us. From the way the housekeeping staff kept our room, to the way the breakfast staff always made sure to take care of us, to the way everyone offered to help as we went in and out with our newborn son ... everything they did was above and beyond the call of duty. Despite how hard it was to live with a newborn out of a hotel room, they did everything they could to make our stay as comfortable as possible.

Hampton Inn at the Kansas City Speedway ... if we are ever in town again, you have more than won our return business. We can say the same about that Famous Dave's. Strangely enough, there was a Church's Chicken up off of Parallel Parkway to the east that also went above and beyond when they heard why we were there. We would call in an order to either of these restaurants and they would prepare everything perfectly, even adding in extras at no charge.

To these three places of business ... we owe you a debt that we simply can't repay.

I was in Target when the call came in. We were approved to go home on January 23rd. The agency got everything done in under a week. Upon returning to the hotel, I booked our return flight with Southwest. The complication was that a winter storm was moving into Denver and that was where our connecting flight was. If there was any kind of weather problem, the trip might be extended. We got up early on the morning of January 24th. On the way to Kansas City International Airport, which is on the Missouri side of the state line, we saw a Bald Eagle fly over the roadway ahead of us.

After boarding, a stewardess said to my wife, "There is no way you just gave birth to your son and look like that." She responded, "Someone else gave birth to him for me." We all laughed. As it would turn out, Aidan slept almost the entire way. Chanthy had to change him on the first leg of the flight from Kansas to Colorado. We were in fact delayed on that first leg, so we had no time to eat lunch at Denver International. We had to run, carrying our bags of baby supplies and a newborn, from flight to flight. It felt like fleeing a war zone, for some reason ... and Chanthy, as a child, did in fact escape the Khmer Rouge killing fields of Cambodia when she herself was an infant. We made the connecting flight just barely and suffered through the lack of lunch.

Frankly, both of us were so tired our bodies didn't really put up a fuss about not eating.

On final approach to Sacramento, we flew just north of Lake Tahoe. There had been a massive series of storms while we were away, and the flight had been quite bumpy over the Rockies and various mountains of the Great Basin. When the ground was visible there was nothing but a thick blanket of white all the way to the Sierra Nevada. I could pick out several of the North Lake Tahoe ski areas as we flew over, blanketed in snow that was obviously abnormally deep. That winter would set records. Meanwhile, turning in the air above Sacramento International, we saw all the flood channels of the Sacramento River filled to the brim. The river was not "flooding" since the excess water was contained in the designated flood channels, but it was quite a sight.

We cried when the wheels hit the ground.

We wandered half-awake but excited through the airport and grabbed our baggage. I went to get the car and brought it around. The drive home was surreal. Our son was with us. We were home. There is a back road that runs from the area of Roseville, California, where we lived at the time, to the airport and we took that instead of the freeway. We were so happy. In our car, my wife rode in the back with our precious cargo. He was sleeping, but would occasionally open his eyes and stare at her the way newborns do. Pulling into the driveway of our home, a home we had just purchased a couple of months earlier, the sense of relief that washed over both of us was palpable.

That night, tired as we were, my parents were passing through town and they stopped by. We got pictures, but we were exhausted. Home at last, now we would begin our new life with our son.

Our dogs took to him immediately. They seemed to sense the gravity of this tiny new life in their midst, and our chihuahua (now nine while Aidan is four) really likes him. She'll often vanish in the evening, and later we discover that she ran to his room so she could sleep near him. It's very sweet.

At the end of the day, including travel expenses, the adoption cost us just over $60,000. That means that in total, including the cost of our fertility treatments, we spent over $149,000 just to have a child. If anyone reading this is going through the profound difficulty and sorrow of infertility ... we feel your pain. There is a light at the end of the tunnel.

Consider adoption.

It may not have been something the reader has considered seriously before. However, there are a large number of children out there who need good homes. Our home has never been the same, and I say that for the better.

Epilogue
Reflections on Life Past, Present, and Future

The past four plus years since bringing Aidan home have been filled with so many emotions. He has grown and is getting so smart. We adopted another dog, bringing our total to three. We go camping, spend time in Tahoe at cabins covered in snow and we go camping and fishing in Mammoth each summer. Well, at least we did prior to the pandemic of 2020. What is life like as the parents of an adopted child? Well, honestly, we imagine that it is much the same as being parents of one's biological child.

One weekend when Aidan was a few months old we were driving out to run some errands. He suddenly turned to my wife sitting next to him, and a huge smile blossomed on his face. He just stared and stared at her smiling ear to ear.

Chanthy, not a daycare center, was the recipient of Aidan's first social smile. This ... all these firsts, is why she decided to be a homemaker.

We have had all of the baby's first moments that other parents have. The love that we have for him is, perhaps, enhanced because it was so difficult for us to become parents to begin with. During those many nights when we awoke over and over for feedings and diaper changes, we smiled. We were losing sleep and going through the hassle ... but we were parents!!! Sorrow had been so overwhelming for us for so many years that losing a little sleep was hardly an inconvenience. Of course, we get frustrated, angry, and go through the normal range of human emotions. But fear that we might never be parents had plagued our daily lives for years, and now we had our precious son. A little poo-nami explosion all over his clothes? Whatever ... we are parents, and we are so full of joy that it just doesn't matter. We'll deal with it.

As for my memories of the Assembly, well, they are an exercise in contrasts. Extreme highs and extreme lows. Perhaps, the best way to capture my memories of those events is to quote the opening sentences of Charles Dickens's legendary work, *A Tale of Two Cities*:

> It was the best of times, it was the worst of times, it was the age of wisdom, it was the age of foolishness, it was the epoch of belief, it was the epoch of incredulity, it was the season of Light, it was the season of Darkness, it was the spring of hope, it was the winter of despair, we had everything before us, we had nothing before us, we were all going direct to Heaven, we were all going direct the other way ...

There are men and women in that group who I called brother and sister in the truest sense of those words. People who I still miss dearly and of whom I have really great memories of time well spent. Then there are others whose coming was like a storm rolling in off the ocean. I lived in constant fear and condemnation regarding my many "sins." I lived in constant hope of an eternal reward to come. There are times when a memory is triggered which brings wistfulness or fondness. There are other times when such memories bring nothing but sorrow and regret. Looking back, more than a decade and a half later, I'm happy where I am with my wife and our son.

After returning from Kansas, that first year progressed. He began sitting. He began scooting. He began crawling. He grew and grew and we smiled and smiled. At left is a family photo we had taken in November 2017. I think the looks on our faces say it all.

Proud.

Happy.

Content.

And our son ... that innocent smile.

Soon after his first birthday he began walking. He was hesitant, but we helped him along and once he started doing it, there was no stopping him. That is his pattern in general. Sometimes he is hesitant to start a new behavior. However, once he starts there is no turning back and he is all in.

Life as parents is amazing. Today, at four, he knows his ABC's, is recognizing that letters can be put together to form words, can count to one hundred and is learning math (he's almost got the base-10 numbering system), is curious about everything and full of questions, and loved trips to the park where he was up and down the slides all day long (was, because, you know ... pandemic). As I type this, we are actually still largely in self-isolation due to the global COVID-19 pandemic. None of us have it (and Chanthy and I have had our vaccines), but we are playing it very safe. We have only just begun going out and taking family trips again, and boy has that been hard. Chanthy, however, is a fabulous cook and really enjoys trying new recipes, and I spend my free time reading, listening to podcasts, and (yes) I still get mileage out of the Xbox.

In mid-2020, we moved into our semi-custom-built dream home not far from our old starter home. The pandemic made this challenging, but we are here to stay and living the dream. All in all, life is very good. We have our struggles as every couple does, and Aidan throws his tantrums and has his growing pains, but I honestly feel like I am married to my dream woman, we have our dream child, and we are living in our dream home ... no god required.

There are many more chapters to be written in the long book of our lives. Today, however, we are contented, healthy, and happy. The future is unknown, but to quote our family saying, we find our hope in our future ... our hope is in imagining a life of adventure experienced together.

Life is good, and, despite all of our history of trials and sorrow, the sun rises each day on a life that is also full of hope.

Acknowledgments

To my dear wife. You have supported me through every single trial we've been through, and we are truly life partners. You are the center of my world, my life, and my joy. Thank you for always believing in me. There is no challenge that we can't overcome together.

To Aidan, my dear son. You won't be able to understand how difficult our journey to have you was for many years, but you understand that you are loved, safe, and happy. That is all that matters to me in this moment.

To Dr. Baljit Atwal, our therapist. You have seen us through so much, and we can't thank you enough for your support.

To my parents, Stan & Karen Conger. You have been my heroes throughout my life. I would not be the man I am today were it not for your loving care and endless support.

About Atmosphere Press

Atmosphere Press is an independent, full-service publisher for excellent books in all genres and for all audiences. Learn more about what we do at atmospherepress.com.

We encourage you to check out some of Atmosphere's latest releases, which are available at Amazon.com and via order from your local bookstore:

The Swing: A Muse's Memoir About Keeping the Artist Alive, by Susan Dennis
Possibilities with Parkinson's: A Fresh Look, by Dr. C
Gaining Altitude - Retirement and Beyond, by Rebecca Milliken
Out and Back: Essays on a Family in Motion, by Elizabeth Templeman
Just Be Honest, by Cindy Yates
You Crazy Vegan: Coming Out as a Vegan Intuitive, by Jessica Ang
Detour: Lose Your Way, Find Your Path, by S. Mariah Rose
To B&B or Not to B&B: Deromanticizing the Dream, by Sue Marko
Convergence: The Interconnection of Extraordinary Experiences, by Barbara Mango and Lynn Miller
Sacred Fool, by Nathan Dean Talamantez
My Place in the Spiral, by Rebecca Beardsall
My Eight Dads, by Mark Kirby
Dinner's Ready! Recipes for Working Moms, by Rebecca Cailor
The Space Between Seconds, by NY Haynes

About the Author

Dan Conger is a Silicon Valley business executive working as an accountant in the medical device industry. *A Walk Through the Wilderness* is his first book, although he has written for his own enjoyment for many years. He enjoys spending time with his family, exploring the outdoors via camping, fishing, hiking, and he and his wife are also avid foodies spending time cooking and constantly trying new recipes. His wife is an amateur photographer and Mr. Conger spends time with her as she pursues her passion. He lives in Rocklin, CA with his wife, son and their three dogs.

Made in the USA
Monee, IL
01 February 2022